The Problem of Moral Rearmament

The Problem
of Moral Rearmament

Poland, the European Union, and the War in Ukraine

CHRISTOPHER GARBOWSKI

WIPF & STOCK · Eugene, Oregon

THE PROBLEM OF MORAL REARMAMENT
Poland, the European Union, and the War in Ukraine

Wipf & Stock
An Imprint of Wipf and Stock Publishers
199 W. 8th Ave., Suite 3
Eugene, OR 97401

www.wipfandstock.com

PAPERBACK ISBN: 979-8-3852-1339-9
HARDCOVER ISBN: 979-8-3852-1340-5
EBOOK ISBN: 979-8-3852-1341-2

04/16/24

Contents

Acknowledgments

IN *HISTORY AND MORALITY* (2022) historian Donald Bloxham argues that historians are entitled to a moral stance in their work. Since it's often present there whether they acknowledge it or not, better for it to be in the open. Although not a work of history as such, in this book it is difficult not have a moral stance living in a country where one lives close to a border across which a horrendous war is taking place. Not only is there the news with all its variations, optimistic and pessimistic, but in Poland there are Ukrainians which you meet in most walks of life, each of them suffering bravely to some degree or another. The question is how this moral stance is integrated in the writing. I started writing about Poland and its response to the war the same year as the war broke out in an article published the following year as "The Ukrainian War: A View from a NATO Eastern Flank Country," in the third number of *The Polish Review* in the 2023 volume. The article constitutes a large portion of the first chapter. I'm grateful to the journal for the possibility of republishing it. Similarly, in 2023 I wrote a number of essays in *Voegelin View* that inspired me with regards to how I should further develop the book I was already writing. Three of these essays in particular I have drawn upon extensively, although with a good deal of editing and interweaving additional research. These are "The Long Road to Ukraine," published February 14; "Cosmopolitan Europe or a Europe of Nations?," published April 2; and "Community and Rituals: A Review of Byung-Chal Han's *The Disappearance of Rituals*," published January 22. I am also grateful to the journal for the possibility of republishing this material. I likewise wish to express my gratitude to Zbigniew Stawrowski for his careful reading of my manuscript and useful comments. Most of all I am grateful to my wife, Monika, for her continual support in this and earlier books.

Introduction

EARLY IN JOHN HUSTON'S classic *African Queen* (1951), forces from the German colonizers come to a small African village, burn it down, and round up the male natives.[1] The brutality is disturbing, and the viewer of the time of release quite possibly thought the filmmaker is indirectly reminding him or her of some of the atrocities the Germans carried out in the more recent war that had just ended a few years before the film was released. But the fact that the Germans have recently paid reparations to Namibia, another one of their African colonies—the colony in which the movie primarily took place is in today's Tanzania, on the other side of the continent—for an act of genocide early in the twentieth century indicates, without digging into the actual history, such cruelty might have been possible.

There is another scene in the movie that is only slightly less shocking. When the protagonists are making their way down the river in the eponymous vessel, they pass a German fort. In that sequence we see Tanzanians next to their European overlords shooting at the protagonists from their vantage point high up in the fort. Early in the film the viewer was informed that that was why the males were rounded up, to augment the German forces in their colony at the beginning of the First World War. From the present perspective, the two scenes together show how history repeats itself, or at least rhymes.

At this juncture in the twenty first century, there are certainly two major colonial powers: the Russians and the Chinese. In the case of the Russians, their full scale invasion of Ukraine early in 2022 was preceded, among others, by a couple of wars in Chechnya in the first decade of the century. That small nation wanted to regain its independence from Russia

1. Huston, *African Queen*.

after the end of the Cold War. Currently, with the courageous resistance of that people cruelly subdued, the Chechens—not to mention citizens of other republics—are now fighting alongside their Russian colonizers against the valiant Ukrainians. Indeed, Chechen leader Ramzan Kadyrov is among Putin's most trusted aides. Much like the recent full scale invasion of Ukraine leading to an influx of the country's refugees to neighboring Poland, there were also refugees to the country from Chechnya earlier in the century: a much smaller number, since the nation has nowhere near the population and is not a direct neighbor. In an interview in the Polish press with one of them during the current war, the refugee called Kadyrov a traitor to his people. Moreover, there is a contingent of them fighting alongside the Ukrainians. This gives some sense that there are many levels to what Chechens are feeling today and likely even in their occupied homeland the Russians are not in full control of their souls.

In this book I primarily look at Poland at the time of the war in Ukraine with great emphasis on the political philosophy and to some extent political theology it has inspired in the country, and the complimentary influence of historical memory on that thought. This focus will primarily pertain to the question of moral rearmament, which will be explained below. Moreover, this will largely follow an initial analysis of the broader sociopolitical background of the country, both in a narrower and broader sense, for these reflections to be better understood.

Poland is a national community that against great historical adversity over the past few centuries has developed a nation state. The national community is likely one of the largest political communities where the term community is not an oxymoron. But the war raises the question of the national community in relation to the transnational polities that create its geopolitical environment. At the most dramatic level, a colonial empire is waging a war with the country that neighbors Poland and it is not out of the question that the invader also can pose a similar threat to its existence at some point in the not altogether distant future.

However, when we speak of empires this raises the question of the status of the European Union of which Poland has been a member since early in the century. That is a complex issue, since the polity is to no small extent a work in progress. As historian Timothy Garton Ash sees it, "Russian President Vladimir Putin's attempt to restore the Russian empire by recolonizing Ukraine has opened the door to a postimperial Europe."[2] He further

2. Ash, "Postimperial Empire."

ponders whether this implies a need for the EU to create a "liberal empire." From another perspective, in his earlier *The Virtue of Nationalism* Israeli scholar Yoram Hazony sees the EU as already an empire: a reconstitution of the German medieval empire, with Germany at its center, and what can be read as a warning to its denizens insists, "Any international federation will be ruled by officials with views of their own as to the appropriate limits that are to be placed on the self-determination of subject nations."[3] Quite contrasting views. In the case of the latter, the "limits" imposed by the EU are one of the issues that the post-Communist member states certainly struggle with, since they not infrequently raise the issue of the national community's sovereignty. In some cases through political means aimed directly at certain seemingly insubordinate countries, in other cases through its rather heavy handed central planning.

One might think for a moment this is not unfamiliar. In his *The Road to Somewhere* of 2017 David Goodhart described a similar situation after Brexit, where he found the underlying division between the "somewheres" and "anywheres" so prevalent in today's world at its root.[4] Goodhart argued that Western society is now composed of "anywheres" and "somewheres." "Anywheres" are the educated, interconnected elites who feel more solidarity with their own transnational caste than with their fellow citizens. The "somewheres" are those who feel an attachment to place, family, and nation.

Nevertheless, the situation in East Central Europe is only partly related to this tension. In the case of Poland the answer is also related to its current sovereignty being only recently regained in historical terms, together with a radically different historical experience of the twentieth century; Nazi fascism was not the only danger that caused the country to suffer—Communism with its universalist socialism encompassed it with an equally totalitarian nightmare, and was much longer lasting. That is why what seems to be a universalist utopianism underpinning the hopes of many EU players rings a number of warning bells among the more conscious denizens of the more recent members of the union: Poland and a number of its neighbors joined the union in 2004 and are still to a great extent regarded—or rather treated—as "new" members.

And as Andrew Michta, an expert at the George C. Marshall European Center for Security Studies, has stated early on Ukraine's stubborn resistance has pushed the importance of national sovereignty "front and center."

3. Hazony, *Virtue of Nationalism*, 154.
4. See Goodhart, *Road to Somewhere*.

Obviously this resistance has been augmented by help from NATO and the EU, but here again the weakness of Europe has been exposed in that, for instance even in April of 2023, despite its similar resources the United States gave twice as much as the continent to help arm the Ukrainians. But once again it must be stressed it is the citizens of a sovereign national community that are courageously defending themselves on the ground. Consequently, too long has the EU relied on soft power and it is stumbling forward to look after the security issue that the war has raised.

In his *The Road to Ukraine* (2022) Frank Furedi raises a crucial matter. The cumulative result of historical amnesia, the neglect of the importance of traditional boundaries, both national and cultural, he insists, has been "the moral disarmament of the West."[5] He continues that as important as rearming the countries of the West may currently be, "what matters now today is not so much military but moral rearmament. . . . Recovering a sense of historical consciousness is the precondition for the Western world to acquire the ability to play a mature and responsible role in global affairs."[6] This problem is a major focus of this book from the perspective of Poland, where there is arguably a degree of moral "armament" and historical memory, but these are suffering for different reasons while actually a considerably fuller measure would serve the national community at such a time. Although in fact it is a problem for virtually each European national community, with its own specificity, but some elements in common.

Among other matters, in Poland moral rearmament can only occur when its resources, such the political philosophy and theology that potentially could promote it, are not restricted to academia. Pertinently, some of the authors whose works I will be exploring do not as such engage in political theology in academia, or rather knowledge factory. Early in this century two political philosophers established the *Political Theology* think tank, which initially published a yearbook and also translations of pertinent classics. Through these and further activities a milieu was created that attracted public intellectuals, scholars, and journalists to contribute to their publications and participate in various events. In their first yearbook, published in 2003, they stated their intent to "look at political matters from the perspective of last things."[7] On their web page they explain their intent to

5. Furedi, *Road to Ukraine*, 92.

6. Furedi, *Road to Ukraine*, 98.

7. Quoted from Cichocki and Karłowicz, "Czym jest Teologia Polityczna," para. 2. The translations from Polish are by the author unless otherwise indicated.

"view social matters from a religious perspective because we are interested in the person as being both *homo politicus* and *homo religious*—one and the same person in the most fundamental dimensions, experiences and needs. The integral nature of both fields is derived from the premise of the integral nature of the person."[8] This is not too different from the most basic definition of political theology, which is "the analysis of political arrangements (including cultural-psychological, social, and economic aspects) from the perspective of God's ways with the world."[9] The Poles interested in this question have their own focus, which at times it is difficult to distinguish from political philosophy. In other words, the political theology I bring to bear on various problems is from a realm primarily governed by political scientists or experts—either from academia or public intellectuals—who wish to reach the broader public sphere from such a perspective, dealing with the present and, fortunately, historical memory.

The situation in Central Europe also brings up another aspect of moral rearmament. When French religious philosopher Chantal Delsol visited Eastern Europe shortly after its countries regained their sovereignty in 1989, she noted the presence of a different sensibility that intrigued her. After some thought, she felt that although at some level "they dreamed of being like us," eventually she felt there was quite a bit to learn there, since "the divergences between us and them led me to the belief that the last fifty years of good fortune had entirely erased our sense of the tragic dimension of life."[10] Later on that sense was also becoming less pronounced in the region, but it was close enough for a marked comeback with the war in Ukraine. A year after the invasion a Polish political philosopher plainly stated the full scale war brought with it what was "not so much an overwhelming, as for many difficult to accept, tragic sense of history."[11] Robert Kaplan helps us understand the broader significance of this sense in his *Tragic Mind* of 2023. Kaplan's reflection on the tragic mind and the meaning of tragedy in politics is quite powerful and timely. He persuasively makes the case that "tragedy begins with the searing awareness of the narrow choices we face, however vast the landscape; the knowledge that not everything is possible,

---

8. Cichocki and Karłowicz, "Czym jest Teologia Polityczna," para. 5.

9. Cavanaugh and Scott, "Introduction," 3.

10. Quoted in Murray, *Strange Death of Europe*, 228.

11. Tokarski, "Bitwa o Europę," 7.

regardless of the conditions."[12] This is the burden of power that the author notes has been inadequately understood in recent years.

In one of the discussions he engaged in after the publication of his earlier *The Revenge of Geography* in 2012, Kaplan astutely observed that with its history and position both within the EU and so close to Russia, Poland's outlook on many matters is affected in a particular manner—a "geographical" context at the center of his book. In his more recent book, he hinted at the truth that goes beyond maps: "The truths of greater interest always involve the province of the heart, in which we drill downward from the map, to culture and accumulated historical experience, to finally the individual."[13]

With the war going on in neighboring Ukraine, this different manner of looking at matters has been strengthened. While sociopolitical concerns are to be examined in this book, "the province of the heart" will be a greater concern: for instance, a national community is also formed by its historical memory, or its lack in some cases. Historical memory certainly invites philosophical reflection, and through its relation to community it can be called history as communion, as one of the functions of history has perceptively been termed.[14] History as communion invites theological reflection, which has also been the case in Poland. But in a fairly obvious manner it can be claimed history has returned to Poland and the rest of Europe. Although it can also be argued that history never left the region. Moreover, radical evil has returned, or to paraphrase Leszek Kołakowski, the devil has returned to history, if he has ever left. This also brings up the question of the ideology that to no small extent propelled and maintains the Russian aggression, which in turn helps us see where Ukraine stands as a national community.

In the book I don't examine the internal situation in Ukraine and the military situation except where it arises in the discussion of Poles or EU members. In the first chapter I primarily briefly examine the effect of the war on Poland, in more detail with regards to the early phase, since at the time of writing the war has still not been concluded, and the beginning has significance for understanding what followed. The second chapter introduces the two empires that form the geopolitical context of this work, the aggressive Russian empire, and the European Union primarily as a

12. Kaplan, *Tragic Mind*, 3.

13. Kaplan, *Tragic Mind*, 2.

14. For a discussion of history as communion, see Bloxham, *Why History?*, 84–94, 314.

normative empire. Ukrainian identity is examined briefly to show how blatantly wrong the Russian propaganda of their target is and give a better idea
of the actual identity of the nation as can be demonstrated from a historical perspective. The first two chapters are primarily sociopolitical in their
analytical scope, and the third chapter analyses several aspects of cultural
and political philosophy in or pertaining to Poland that will also be augmented by political theology, to no small degree focused on the problem of
the moral rearmament of the country that Furedi persuasively insists is so
important at this time, and so through the context of the war. And thus the
existing historical memory in Poland that explains the survival of a tragic
sensibility is a counter to the historical amnesia Furedi determined as a
deterrent to this axiological task, and plays an important part in a deeper
reflection of the present dangerous times.

1

The Ukrainian War in Its Early Stages

A View from Neighboring Poland

IN HIS ARTICLE ON the brutality of Russian soldiers in the Ukraine after their invasion on February 24, 2022, Christopher Szabo relates how the behavior of those soldiers reminded him of growing up in Pretoria in the 1970s and listening to stories from Hungarian, East German, and Polish refugees about the Red Army "liberating" their countries. He brings up his mother's account of "the Red Army's entry into Budaörs [Hungary], and of how young women like herself dressed as grandmothers and avoided the Soviet soldiers' gaze, as well as friends who were raped." He continues: "this made me begin to wonder, 'why doesn't anyone care about this?'"[1]

Part of his answer might be found in the reflection of Toomas Hendrik Ilves, a former president of Estonia, who summed up some of the responses he met with before the current Ukrainian war from politicians from neighboring Scandinavian countries in the EU when he voiced his concerns on the potential threat from Russia: "The only people in the world toward whom it is politically correct to behave like a racist is toward Eastern Europeans. You are not allowed to criticize the Russians, because this will be called Russophobia, but regarding Eastern Europe everything is allowed."[2]

In Poland, already in 2020 literary scholar Antoni Libera noted the development of Putin's imperial scheme had been initiated quite clearly

---

1. Szabo, "Why Have the Russians," para. 22.
2. Ilves and Dutczak, "Były prezydent Estonii," para. 2.

already back in 2007, when he complained that the fall of the Soviet Union was Russia's greatest tragedy and how he imagined himself destined to correct the situation. In his essay, Libera wrote that the Russian president imagined himself carrying out Peter the Great's vision, in which Russia bordered on Germany—and shortly after current the invasion Putin indeed compared himself to the tsar. Moreover, the dictator had no respect for the West. "Vladimir Putin," Libera writes, "is aware (like few others in the world) that a civilization incapable of sacrifices is in the position of a loser, while one that is ready to make sacrifices has the possibility of victory."[3]

As has been made apparent, Putin challenged the West in this manner, that is with the acceptance of tremendous sacrifices, when he pulled out all the stops in his—actually second[4]—invasion of Ukraine. Initially it seemed the West was united but significant differences soon appeared. Timothy Snyder had to put it plainly for those who had difficulty in discerning the basic facts of what had happened: the Russian invasion of their neighbor was a colonial war.[5] Snyder also provides a pithy historical background of the invasion, that despite its brevity goes considerably beyond the importance of the earlier invasion of Ukraine and annexation of Crimea by the Russians in 2014.

Andrew Michta drew a conclusion from this very perspective on the event: as was mentioned in the introduction, he noted Ukraine's stubborn resistance has pushed the importance of national sovereignty "front and center." "After three decades of post-Cold War institutionalism and globalism," he emphasizes that "we are back to the fundamentals of national security: only a sovereign Ukraine can provide its citizens with a secure homeland." He further noted that international institutions could not stop Russia from invading Ukraine. Consequently, "there is no substitute for hard power, and no nation can remain secure if it lacks a strong military, regardless of whether or not it belongs to a military alliance, for NATO has yet again defaulted to the United States to secure Europe."[6] Michta argued peace should not always be the first priority in a conflict: Putin earlier demonstrated that a peace settlement would likely be a tactic on his part to prepare for a future attack. Thus, "As Ukrainians have shown us when

---

3. Libera, "Widmo rozbioru," para. 10.

4. For a thorough account of the first invasion of Ukraine, its roots and consequences, see Yekelchyk, *Conflict in Ukraine*.

5. Snyder, "War in Ukraine."

6. Michta, "Russia's Invasion of Ukraine," 2.

attacked, the goal should not be to reach a compromise as soon as possible, but to defeat the aggressor and liberate the nation's territory."[7] Half a decade before the second invasion, while many in the West were coming to terms with the hybrid war that continued, James Kirchick insightfully claimed, "Ukraine's fate is about far more than the destiny of one former Soviet republic; it concerns the destiny of Russia, Europe, and the universal right of self-determination."[8] In his speech before the Ukrainian parliament in May after the invasion President Andrzej Duda put it simply: "The free world today has the face of Ukraine."[9]

One might add to the above that in light of the Russian aggression, Poland, which had been seen as Russophobic along the lines the former president of Estonia complained of, was finally acknowledged as having been right in its concerns. As Elisabeth Shaw of the American Enterprise Institute put it, around the time of President Joe Biden's visit to the country in March 2022, former Soviet Bloc countries saw the threat more clearly, while Western European countries had to admit their view of Russia was misguided.[10] It also seemed for a while that this foresight of Poland and some of the countries in East Central Europe were now about to be rewarded for this. In an opinion piece at the time for *Politico* entitled "Europe's East Gets Its Day," Jeremie Gallon boldly stated, "The time when Paris and Berlin alone could decide the Continent's future is over. In this newly emerging phase, it is the countries of Eastern and Central Europe that will have growing influence."[11]

In this introductory chapter, I explore the overall Polish perspective together with the country's initial response to the war in Ukraine. This is primarily limited to some key aspects of how the war affected Polish society at that point in time, that is approximately the first half year of the conflict, which at the time of writing, it seems, will not be concluded any time soon, with the end result up in the air and far from optimistic. Some later developments are briefly covered toward the end of the chapter and in appropriate parts of the book. Social consequences such as the flood of refugees from the war-torn country to Poland are among those covered. In its position as a NATO eastern flank country, Poland had particular interest in

7. Michta, "Russia's Invasion of Ukraine," para. 2.

8. Kirchick, *End of Europe*, 211.

9. For the entire speech, see Duda, "Przemówienie prezydenta Andrzeja Dudy," para. 5.

10. Lovett, "Poland Warned."

11. Gallon, "Europe's East Gets its Day," para. 2.

the organization's summit in Madrid at the end of June 2022. Moreover, the acceptance of the candidacy of Ukraine as a potential member in the EU, which was a key for the nation's fighting morale as the conflict persisted, led to a rather fecund discussion in Poland that on some points merged with the discussion on the results of the NATO summit. Some further developments are also briefly discussed.

The initial outpouring of support in Poland for Ukrainians under attack was tremendous and also evoked a response at the symbolic level. Many institutions, for instance universities, hung Polish and Ukrainian flags together in a gesture of solidarity. For a time signs of *Slava Ukraini* (Glory to Ukraine) were often alongside these. One might add that even in a speech given at the University of Warsaw in May, the US Ambassador to the country, Mark Brzezinski, used the phrase. In that speech he also pointed out, "Many countries opened their borders for Ukrainians, nevertheless Poland is the leader, creating a safe space for each refugee from Ukraine."[12]

Doubtlessly, the greatest sign of solidarity of Poles with Ukraine was the acceptance of the flood of refugees from the attacked country. According to information given by the Polish Border Guard agency, over four and a half million refugees fleeing the Russian invasion crossed the border from Ukraine into Poland by Friday, July 9.[13] In a report published by the Polish Institute of Economics (PIE), during the first three months after the war, the stages of the involvement are succinctly described: "At the start, spontaneous help dominated: grassroots initiatives by the Polish public, a massive and rapid social effort of an unprecedented nature, supported by local government bodies and the central authorities. During the next stage, adaptation, the role of the state increased and the role of civil society decreased."[14] In the month following the outbreak of war, in March the Polish government enacted a measure offering wide-ranging support to Ukrainians. Many of these Ukrainians left for other countries and most of the men returned to their country to participate in the resistance to the invaders, which largely accounts for the 2.68 million that left for their homeland. From relatively early on, Ukrainian men needed special permission to leave their country. What is unknown was how often refugees from safe areas travelled back and forth a number of times to take care of pertinent matters. These cases undoubtedly also affected the statistics somewhat.

12. See Brzezinski, "Pomoc, którą wspólnie ofiarujemy," 3.
13. "Poland Welcomes 4.62 Million Refugees."
14. Baszczak et. al. *How Polish Society*, 6.

Another matter was how the refugees felt about their stay in the country. For instance, a woman might have intended to eventually return to Ukraine but learned that her husband died at the front and her whole life changed.

The experience of becoming a refugee was certainly traumatic for Ukrainians. Here is the account of a photographer from Kyiv who arrived in Krakow a few days after the war broke out:

> The moment I felt myself to be a refugee was when we got off our evacuation train in Krakow. There were two thousand of us. We got out on the platform with all our things, and there—cameras, reporters. And here you are in such a terrible state, you wanted to hide from these cameras. . . . There are these huge tents where you have to register, they give a sandwich, hot tea. Some older fellow noticed I have a cat, and he brought me two bags of cat food. When he gave them to me, I felt like a refugee I had earlier only seen on television![15]

As this example indicates, this initial influx was met with a highly supportive response on the part of Poles; over half a million refugees were taken into their own homes.[16] According to the authors of the PIE report it was estimated three quarters of the Polish society was involved in some form of direct support of the refugees, whether in fund raising, helping find places to stay, in dealing with administrative questions, etc.[17] Taking into account their number, the corresponding response of Ukrainians who were working or studying in the country was comparatively even greater. Significantly, because of this combined response there were very few refugee camps. Jan Rulewski, an activist during the original Solidarity movement, claimed the welcome was a natural Polish response: "Poles have empathized with those who were attacked, which is why the underhandedness and barbarity of the Russians moved us so much. It is our *non possumus* for treacherous Russia."[18] He himself is sorry that the current Solidarity trade union had not participated significantly in this support of the refugees, but now Ukrainians themselves experience solidarity in Poland. Rulewski's opinion indicates that in part the humanitarian outpouring in recent months on the part of Poles toward their eastern neighbors in dire straits had a patriotic component directed against an aggressor they knew all too well from their

---

15. Quoted in Kari, "Siła dobroci i siostrzeństwa," para. 1.

16. See, for instance, Brzezinski, "Pomoc, którą wspólnie ofiarujemy," 3.

17. Baszczak, et. al., *How Polish Society*, 6.

18. Rulewski, "Warto mieć takiego sąsiada," 7.

own history. Indeed, among the funds raised by NGOs and religious groups to support Ukrainians, one collection was directed at buying a Turkish drone for their combat efforts.

The help for the refugees came in various forms. It started in reception centers organized near border crossings. The Lublin Voivodeship, for instance, had four such centers. But there were numerous grassroots groups, especially in large cities, where social media was used to organize help. A journalist noticed that this altruistic activity created social capital among Poles themselves. Someone may have practically ignored a neighbor from the same apartment building and discovered that he was a professional driver who in his spare time delivered packages with donated goods to a neighborhood center for refugees. It also brought Poles closer to Ukrainians. The journalist related how he talked to a volunteer at a reception center close to the border. The man informed him that all the goods he had for Ukrainians were gathered from his neighbors in the district. "So I understand this is a form of neighborly cooperation?" the journalist asked, referring to people the volunteer knew from the vicinity, to which the volunteer responded in a revealing manner: "Yes, after all, the Ukrainians have been our neighbors for years."[19] Obviously this overwhelmingly positive response does not mean that there were no negative incidents, and at times these were used to criticize Polish authorities. Moreover, even within the Ukrainian community that had been in Poland for a longer period of time and are the most engaged volunteers, there were those who abstained from contributing their time, to the chagrin of the rest of the community.

Of particular importance has been the help and support the Catholic Church and its faithful have offered the multitude of refugees after the outbreak of the war. The entire community at its different levels has been engaged in this support: from Caritas, the charity organization of the episcopate—the largest such organization in the country—through religious orders, as well as the various Catholic groups. There is hardly a parish in the country that has not offered assistance to victims of the war in Ukraine.[20]

The Polish state supported the refugees who stayed in the country in various ways. They initially received free public transport, health care, and their children could attend public schools, while Poles who took in refugees eventually received a subsidy per each person, among others things. Poland spent an estimated €8.36 billion on maintaining refugees from Ukraine in

19. Dobrołowicz, "Nie zostawaj w domu," 17.
20. Przeciszewski, *Kościół w Polsce 2023*.

2022, the highest figure among the member countries of the Organisation for Economic Co-operation and Development (OECD), according to the organization's publication on migration.[21] In that first year by October the EU contributed a fraction of this cost, €144.6 million to help it deal with the huge wave of refugees fleeing Ukraine. As one journalist put it at the time, "Up until now the European Union has done everything to confirm its image of an ideological bureaucratic machine unable to face up to genuine challenges and refuses to put into motion adequate financial means."[22] This attitude toward broader EU insensitivity on this account is common enough in much of East Central Europe; as Slovenian politician Žiga Turk put it, "particularly now, when Poland is literally on the frontline and accepting millions of Ukrainian refugees, the virtue-signaling resolution of March 10 of the European parliament, asking the Commission to punish Poland and Hungary for their democratic transgressions was not timed well."[23]

Most of the member states of the EU are also members of NATO. The organization held a summit in Madrid at the end of June, where the topic of the war in Ukraine was naturally uppermost. And since the eastern flank countries were geographically so close to the conflagration—in its scope unlike any other war in Europe since World War II—there were security implications for these countries that concerned NATO. At the summit the Russian war of aggression against Ukraine was condemned and declared a blatant violation of international law, in which "Russia's appalling cruelty has caused immense human suffering and massive displacements, disproportionately affecting women and children. Russia bears full responsibility for this humanitarian catastrophe."[24]

Among the more practical results of the summit was the acceptance of the applications of Finland and Sweden for membership in NATO: however, at first Turkey only withdrew its initial objection for Finland, only doing so for Sweden after quite some time. Both countries had been horrified by the full-scale invasion of Ukraine. This extends the border of members of the organization with Russia by 1,340 kilometers. More importantly for the eastern flank nations, this means that together with the Baltic states that had been admitted to NATO in 2002, the Baltic Sea would now be

---

21. Kononczuk, "EU Has Given Poland €145m."
22. Woziński, "Wojenny rachunek," 15.
23. Turk, "'Ever Closer' Union," para. 12.
24. "Madrid Summit Declaration," para. 3.

surrounded by the organization's members, which is crucial in any potential direct confrontation with Russia.

The alliance is also supposed to become capable of presenting a quick reaction force of three hundred thousand soldiers, which some claim should be sufficient to defend all NATO territory in Central and Northern Europe. But much depends on how quickly this force can be organized. There was also a decision to install the headquarters of the US Army Fifth Corps in Poznań. Unfortunately, this does not include a permanent presence of American troops in Poland; formally American troops remain stationed in the country on a rotational basis.

Although the alliance condemned the Russian invasion, it nonetheless maintained the NATO-Russian Founding Act from 1997, a form of treaty with the country when it was expected relations would improve. This, as director of the Polish Institute of International Affairs Sławomir Dębski argued, was inconceivable: "Russia has broken all possible conditions of the act, yet some members of the alliance feel it might still be of use, which means, to make it clear, building politics on the basis of an illusion, and not the reality we have to deal with."[25]

Where do the roots of the problem lie? Dębski argues it is with European politics. Although brought up in the context of the Madrid summit, one could add it was the further result of an ongoing problem. More than a month before the summit Paul Krugman of the *New York Times* argued that Putin's war of aggression was running on money gained from selling fossil fuels to Europe, and despite Ukraine's heroic effort if this dependence was not ended the tyrant wouldn't be stopped. Krugman laid the blame most heavily on Germany—"whose political and business leaders insist they can't do without Russian natural gas, even though many of its own economists disagree—has in effect become Putin's prime enabler."[26] On the topic of Western European dependence on natural gas from Russia, another factor that contributed to it was that shale gas exploitation, despite apparently rich deposits in the continent, was abandoned for ecological reasons. Is it surprising that conservation groups received money from the Russian government—eighty two million euros—to augment their campaigns?[27]

---

25. Dębski, "Zachód bardziej boi się przegranej," para. 12.

26. Krugman, "How Germany Became Putin's Enabler," para. 2.

27. Głuchowski, "Kto zdjął nogę z gazu."

In a similar tone to Krugman's with regards to Germany, *Politico* journalist Matthew Karnitschnig argued Germans acted as Putin's "useful idiots" for years:

> Germany's stubborn insistence on engaging with the Russian leader in the face of his sustained aggression (a catalog of misdeeds ranging from the invasion of Georgia to assassinations of enemies abroad and war crimes in Syria) was nothing short of a catastrophic blunder, one that will earn Merkel a place in the pantheon of political naiveté alongside Neville Chamberlain.[28]

Dębski argued the results of this foot dragging in arming the Ukrainians and the naive dialogue with Putin were a much larger number of deaths of the soldiers defending their country and decreasing its chances of victory. This largely continued after the summit. As Dębski ironically noted, "It seems the West is more afraid of Russia losing than Ukraine losing."[29] And the Germans were merely the worst in this regard of "enabling" Putin, but they were hardly alone. One Polish pundit claimed, "'Old' Europe offers Ukraine solidarity, but it is not a fighting solidarity, merely one that maintains appearances. It wants to return as soon as possible to a world of appearances: appearances of security and progress."[30] This world of appearances is troubling not only for Ukraine, but also for eastern flank NATO countries like Poland at a much closer proximity to the aggressor's potential renewal of furies if it were merely "appeased" at present. To put it another way, the EU remains essentially a soft power, and in the current situation of war this is not enough to ensure the security of its members. And the countries of Central Europe are mostly aware of this fact. The amendment of this condition is quite slow and shall be discussed in the next chapter.

But at least Poland was aware of the energy problems well in advance of the war and became independent of Russian gas. As Jeffrey Sonnenfeld put it, Poland almost completely eliminated all dependence on Russian piped gas. He claimed "that the challenge of European dependence on Russian energy is a challenge of political willpower, not technical constraints, supply limitations, or esoteric geology." Sonnenfeld argued this comes down "to the willingness of political leaders to lead. Poland's pivot towards gas sovereignty was wrought by several leaders who had the courage to make

28. Karnitschnig, "Putin's Useful German Idiots," para. 7.

29. Dębski, "Zachód bardziej boi się przegranej."

30. Nowak, "Granice Europy," 81.

unpopular and even controversial decisions that have proven prescient in hindsight."[31]

A couple of weeks before the Madrid Summit Ukraine was granted candidate status for potential EU membership. This is the first case of a country engaged in a full scale war receiving this status. The Polish government lobbied on behalf of the country for some time but to little avail. What turned the tables, according to Polish journalist Jędrzej Bielecki, was the forceful attitude of Ursula von der Leyen, the head of the European Commission.[32] Inspired by the earlier path breaking visit of both the Polish prime minster and president to President Zelensky in Kiev, von der Leyen herself visited him on June 11. After surveying what was happening, she announced that the EC would recommend the status. Forced by this visit and announcement, the heads of state Chancellor Olaf Scholz, President Emmanuel Macron, and Italian prime minister Mario Draghi likewise visited Kiev, announcing they would support the candidacy. A couple of days later at the meeting of the heads of state of the EU on the twenty-third of June it was indeed accepted. The road from candidacy to EU membership is long; for Poland it was fifteen years. But what is crucial for the Ukrainians is that it gave them additional motivation to continue the long and exhausting war effort and would likely have had the opposite effect had it been rejected, as it was at an earlier summit.

The contribution to the war effort by Poles was enormous. Sufficient to mention that the value of their contribution for military support in the first months was roughly the equivalent to that of the Germans despite the huge difference in GNP to the benefit of the latter. Poland also acted as a major hub for the transfer of military aid to Ukrainians from different sources. Even the intake of refugees had a partial military sense in that the men at the front from particularly vulnerable areas whose wives and children were in Poland were more confident that nothing would happen to their loved ones while they were absent from home, and so their morale for combat was higher.

Worth noting for the first few months of the war there was a fairly good personal relationship between Polish President Duda and President Zelenski. Realizing a crisis was brewing—both parties had information from the Americans that something ugly was brewing—the Polish president invited his Ukrainian counterpart to his private residence in Poland in what turned

31. Sonnenfeld, "Poland Was Right," para. 7.
32. Bielecki, "O przyszłości Unii zdecyduje Ukraina," 10.

out to be very shortly before the invasion took place. This was a gesture that was supposed to make it easier for them to work together in case of an emergency, and for a time indeed had that effect. This is perhaps not so unusual since despite some problems Polish-Ukrainian relations steadily progressed since the neighboring country declared independence in 1991—indeed Poland was the first country to recognize Ukrainian independence.

In recognition of the special help on so many fronts that the Polish government had conveyed to Ukrainians since the onset invasion, President Zelenski sent a bill in early July to the Ukrainian parliament to confer upon Polish citizens staying in Ukraine similar privileges to those that the country's refugees have had in Poland. Moreover, at a symbolic level the cities of Przemyśl and Rzeszów were granted the honorary title of city-lifeguards. Polish-Ukrainian relations had never been so strong. But the natural question that arose is what is their potential, assuming a worst case scenario does not occur in the war and Ukrainians maintain at least more or less the current level of their sovereignty and territory.

This question was considered quite early by Polish experts from various think tanks. Among the bolder ideas that have been laid out was that of Marek Budzisz, a journalist, businessman, and expert at strategy and future, an independent think tank. In his column for an online journal he examined the military situation of the time and some of the responses of Ukrainian politicians, among them from one politician who had been negatively disposed toward Poles before the war but now saw matters in a different light. Among other things the politician noted moments in history when Poles and Ukrainians cooperated to their mutual advantage, suggesting a road forward. In view of such transformations Budzisz felt that a key historical juncture was approaching in the relations between the two nations that required bold long term thinking. He suggested something along the lines of working towards a federation binding the two states.[33]

Budzisz was not alone in such thinking, and in a number of variations the debate continued for some time, so it is worth presenting the initial stage in greater detail. As was to be expected the original idea was considered too bold by some commentators. Michał Steć of the Jagiellonian Club, a Republican think tank, argued that among other things such a solution did not take into account the fact that Ukrainians were asserting their own identity through the war and on their part such a federation would mean giving up quite a bit of that to the partner in a somewhat stronger position.

33. Budzisz, "Pora na postawienie kwestii."

Moreover, the two nations are too different, especially through their diverse experiences of Communism and post-Communism.[34] As Serhy Yekelchyk noted, "As a graduate student in 1989–1991, I saw the Polish example as something Ukraine would not be able to emulate any time soon. Poles won their freedom precisely because they were so un-Soviet, so certain of their national identity. This conviction produced a strong civil society that could rebuild Poland after the fall of communism."[35] One might add, among other reasons, through their EU membership Poland was motivated to deal with the corruption that had permeated Communist societies and that stuck to them even after the system had broken down, and by some counts Ukrainians are still dealing with.[36] As Krzysztof Mularczyk puts it, "The lack of oligarchy cannot be underestimated. There has been petty corruption, nepotism and cronyism in Poland, but no oligarchy. Compared with places like Russia, Ukraine and the Balkan countries, Poland has no oligarchs."[37] Therefore Poland is considerably higher up the list in Transparency International. Unlike Budzisz initially, Steć was writing his comments after Ukraine had gained EU candidacy status.

Budzisz did not respond directly to his critics but in an influential podcast interview he was asked to respond to some of the criticisms,[38] which included points raised by Steć. He claimed that with regards to the term federation he had used, it was less important than that the countries move toward some genuine closer alliance; something along the lines of what Germany and France arranged and developed for themselves after World War II. Poland could become a hub in a different sense than now, among other things helping Ukrainians meet the expectations of EU candidates for membership. This would require realism on the part of Ukrainians, for instance it would entail awareness of the lengthy struggle ahead. Budzisz cited a survey taken shortly after their candidacy was announced and the results revealed a highly unrealistic sense by many Ukrainians of how long it would take to become actual members. They believed they could become members within five years. This manner of thinking could lead to great

---

34. Steć, "Rzeczpospolita Narodów Polski i Ukrainy?"

35. Yekelchyk, "Homage to Poland," para. 4.

36. For an analysis of why some post-Communist countries like Poland managed to advance while others continued to have serious problems and even regress for a time, like Ukraine, see Ghodsee and Orenstein, *Taking Stock of Shock*. For a detailed analysis of why Poland made such significant economic strides, see Piatkowski, *Europe's Growth Champion*.

37. Mularczyk, "Poland Has Remained," para. 14.

38. Janke and Budzisz, "Federacja, ścisła współpraca czy dystans?"

disappointment among the population down the road, after it became obvious how naive it had been, and would have to be dealt with to not cause additional problems. In this and in other such matters Poles could help.

One of the points in which Budzisz was in line with Steć was in the question of taking advantage of Ukrainian military experience. Through the war the latter gained a great deal of experience that at a strategic level could help modernize the overly hierarchical Polish army. In other words, one might add, modernizing national security means something beyond stocking up on the most advanced arms, as necessary as those may be for an eastern flank NATO country.[39] And this discussion was part of the question others have raised about the preparedness of Poland to face a Russian attack as effectively as Ukraine had. It has been noted that even if NATO can be counted on, for some time Poles would have to deal with the attack by themselves, and Russians would likely have learned from their earlier mistakes, which is indeed becoming more and more visible. A much greater degree of militarization of Polish society is called for, that might involve, for instance, a national military draft and the creation of a national reserve army and all that entails. The example of Finland has been brought up, a country that has a general draft and resultant reserve army despite the liberal nature of its society—something that the proximity to Russia had convinced them was necessary quite some time earlier. However, such an overall effort would require Polish society rising above its internal divisions, which have become as intense as in many Western societies.[40] Moreover, the close proximity of war has not decreased postelection tensions, demonstrating it is more than a cultural war. It is worth adding, that the former minister of defense in Poland started increasing the size of army—as well as increasing military preparedness—but even though Poles are generally more patriotic than most EU countries a sizeable portion of the population were against a general military draft, and the continuing horrors of the war are not without effect.

Budzisz indicated there were those who claimed aiming for such increased proximity of Poland to Ukraine would draw the aggression of the Russians. His answer to this was that regardless of whether such an alliance exists or not aggression would likely be directed at Poland once

---

39. Naturally Poland increased its spending on defense. The results of this were discussed in Karnitschinig and Kość, "Meet Europe's Coming Military Superpower."

40. For a discussion of the specificity of the current divisions within Polish society, see Staniszewski, *Polska wojna kulturowa*.

Russia eventually regained its strength, no matter how much it would be weakened by this war. After all, the Russians would undoubtedly wish to punish Poles for their support, an early major factor that provided their neighbors a chance against their aggressors. And it would be better if Poles and Ukrainians were responding together at such a point in the future if it were to occur.

Another matter that had been brought up by Steć was the probability of the historical dark cards in Ukrainian-Polish relations causing problems for some Poles.[41] This genuine issue was not responded to by Budzisz, but it can be looked at a number of ways. I will first indicate a symbolic moment that pertains to Poland, but has significance also for Ukraine. In the late eighteenth century the large Polish Lithuanian Commonwealth was partitioned among three regional powers, including the Russian empire; thus its voting citizens—for that historical period a large body—lost their sovereign state. The Poles in exile later saw what seemed an opportunity when Napoleon ravaged these partitioning powers and so they served the Frenchman gaining some benefits for their cause while he advanced in the pertinent part of the Europe of the day. But they had to pay the piper. Among other things, he ignominiously sent Polish soldiers to Saint Domingue to crush a slave uprising. Fortunately they failed. But over the course of centuries, a number of historical power brokers played similar games taking advantage of different disempowered Central European national groups yearning for sovereignty. Unfortunately this included Ukrainian groups in the service of Hitler. This is the grain of truth in Putin's heinous propaganda that he is "denazifying" Ukraine.

It is worth drawing upon what a Ukrainian author had to say on the matter. Political scientist Georgiy Kasianov does not deny this problem and other darker moments in his nation's history. He also forcefully responds to the historical politics of Putin: "Both Russia and Ukraine are obsessed with the past and are guilty of distorting the historical record for modern purposes." Nevertheless, he poignantly insists, that "there is a fundamental difference in their positions." By this he means their use of history in the war: "Russia turns to the past to justify expansion, aggression, and domination, to resurrect an empire. Ukraine does it in self-defense and

---

41. For an account of the darkest of these historical problems, see Snyder, *Reconstruction of Nations*, 154–78. There are also problems along these lines between Ukrainians and Jews for similar historical reasons. These are presented by Ruth R. Wisse and placed in the context of the positive change the author saw in the renewed nation: see Wisse, "Zelensky the Jewish Hero,"15–19.

self-determination to preserve and nurture an independent republic. Russia fights for the past. Ukraine fights for the future."[42] One might add Ukrainians have largely evolved an inclusive civic patriotism in the last decades.

And that fight for the future continues: obviously the mounting casualties have an effect on the spirit of the Ukrainians in their defensive warfare, while the Russians, seemingly heedless of their own much higher casualties, commit war crime after war crime—arguably attaining genocidal stature—when the occasion arises. Bucha, among the earliest, became a symbol of these. Moreover, the infrastructure of Ukraine is repeatedly attacked: despite enormous ingenuity on the part of Ukrainians,[43] problems such as many homes without heating in the winter are to be the norm, already experienced once, likely again. In November 2022 NATO additionally deemed Russia a "terrorist state," calling on its member states to intensify support of Ukraine.[44] While Putin himself was issued an arrest warrant by the international criminal court in The Hague a few months later.

A pithy summary of the situation outside of the war zone and Poland's role several months after the early period primarily covered in this chapter can be found in an article that Michael Fallon wrote for the British newspaper *The Telegraph* in November 2022, and so a view from the outside. Fallon headed the Ministry of Defence for several years under David Cameron and Theresa May. He begins, "Britain has been steadfast, supplying training, weapons and strong political support. The United States, as always, has done the heaviest lifting of all, spending over USD 18 billion on munitions and other military equipment. But Ukraine's truest friend is Poland."[45] Poland has taken in a disproportionate share of Ukrainian refugees and its economy has suffered the greatest hit, with GDP growth falling from 4 percent to 1.6 percent in 2022, and "it's Poland that has unstintingly raided its own inventories to give Ukrainian troops the weapons that they desperately need to defend their homeland." He adds that Poland should shame its Western allies into doing more to help:

> Nearly eight million Ukrainians have crossed the border into Poland since February; over 20,000 more still arrive every day. They're fed, housed, and given free travel and places in school for their children. Families across Poland have opened their doors to

42. Kasianov, "War over Ukrainian Identity."
43. Dettmer, "Key Weapons in Ukraine's Resilience," paras. 1–6.
44. Gupta, "NATO Deems Russia 'Terrorist State.'"
45. Fallon, "Vladimir Putin Is Becoming Desperate," para. 1.

the biggest movement of people on our continent since the Second World War.[46]

He goes on to inform that Poland would spend a staggering €8.4 billion on helping their Ukrainian refugees that year, while only receiving a contribution of only €144 million from the EU. Moreover, Poland's wealthier western neighbors were not contributing as much to the war effort and that the country granted more military aid to Ukraine than any other EU country, four times more than France, while Germany continued to "drags its feet" despite promises. In other words, what can be concluded is that while more or less important details can be added, essential elements of the first six months were still discernible after a number of additional months had passed. However, Poland only had limited resources so this vivid picture was to change, at least in term of the larger picture.

Moreover, as experts have informed a broader public, defense is easier in warfare than offence. Despite surprising the world that it withstood the initial onslaught and managed some additional early successes, although progress was made in the counteroffensive in the summer of 2023, it did not meet Ukrainian expectations. And it soon became obvious that despite heavy losses, the Russians kept drawing on their enormous human reserves, waiting for both Ukrainians to become exhausted and lose their zeal, and their supporters to become less enthusiastic or unable to keep supplying them with much needed weapons and equipment. The NATO Vilnius summit in July of that year was hardly positive, as we shall see. And certainly the Ukrainians suffered heavy losses at the front, with resources of all kinds being strained, for instance first aid on the front. Whereas in the early period of the war Ukrainians volunteered to fight, as the conflict continued and casualties mounted, a draft became necessary to maintain the armed resistance. And, as Ilya Shablinsky puts in the *Rights in Russia* blog, in October of 2023 Putin was "quite happy with himself and the situation at the front. He has adjusted to the new strategy, to wage a long defensive (for now) war of attrition and to wait . . . for general fatigue in Europe."[47] Moreover, after Hamas provoked a major war in October 2023, interest in Ukraine did wane significantly. Symbolically, shortly after the attack Russian officials welcomed Hamas leaders to Moscow.

As time passes and the war continues, even the staunchest allies have their disagreements. Unlike the Russians, both the Poles and Ukrainians

---

46. Fallon, "Vladimir Putin Is Becoming Desperate," para. 8.

47. Shablinsky, "It's the Same Old Story," para. 4.

are a part of national communities that have been both strengthened and constrained by democratic politics. Electorates have to be heeded and their needs somehow addressed. A crisis came about in the summer of 2023. Right from the beginning of the war the Russians struck at the Ukrainian economy by blocking shipments of their grain largely to developing countries through the Black Sea—in 2014 they had taken over Crimea, which allowed them to control shipping there. So the alternative was to transport the grain through the EU, but understandably the Ukrainians also hoped to sell their grain there. Unfortunately, the ruling party in Poland at the time was preparing for an election, and the farmers were against importing the cheap grain of their neighbors, among others since with the heavy EU regulations and higher cost of living in Poland raising their expenses they could not compete. The ruling party bowed to the demands of one of its key electorates. Oleksii Arestovych, former adviser to Zelensky, said both national parties played the crisis poorly, albeit for different reasons.[48] This was among the earliest of major criticisms of the Ukrainian president's politics during the war. Arestovych also intends to run against Zelensky in the presidential elections of 2024 if the war does not prevent them from taking place. The new Polish government, on the other hand, continues augmenting the divisions in Polish society.

Other problems include the slow rearmament of European countries and a number of them, including Poland at the time of writing, for a time ran out of arms they could pass on to the Ukrainians. Moreover, the Americans stopped their shipment of arms in late 2023. This together with other mounting negative developments could have serious consequences. In November 2023 deputy director at the Council on Geostrategy in London Gabriel Elefteriu, for instance, looks at the arms producing capability of Russians and concludes that for twenty months "the West has been churning out hopeful readings of Ukraine's situation together with broadly dismissive analyses of Russia's warfighting capacity."[49] Some of these problems regarding Europe we will look at more closely in the next chapter.

There are obviously a number of negative scenarios that are possible. For instance, a negotiated ceasefire in which Russia is allowed to keep some of its gains, thus being able to save face—but it is feared this would also provide the regime with enormous propaganda tools, both at home and abroad, and possibly the resumption of economic ties with Western

48. Arestovych, "Zełenski uwierzył, że rządzi światem," 82–84.
49. Elefteriu, "Ukraine War," para. 36.

countries, some of which are still present. While a dispirited Ukraine would quite possibly have internal problems galore, both economic and social. Even assuming a relatively positive outcome of the war with the end of hostilities, obviously Ukraine will require enormous help with recovery. The EU has promised to help finance the operation—it has already been assisting in financing the exhausted state, but even here there are problems. Poland will no doubt be involved in some manner. Then there is Marek Budzisz's idea of a closer association between the two countries to their mutual benefit. Interestingly enough, Dalibor Rohac, an expert from the American Enterprise Institute, thought in similar terms, recalling the co-operation between the national communities during the Polish Lithuanian Commonwealth. He even proposes a fairly strong bond. Among other arguments he suggested a year after the war broke out: "The Polish-Ukrainian Union would become the second-largest country in the EU and arguably its largest military power, providing more than an adequate counterweight to the French-German tandem—something that the EU is sorely missing after Brexit."[50] From the Ukrainian side, in the fall of 2023 Arestovych similarly argued that at the conclusion of the war for the Poles and Ukrainians a closer security agreement would be beneficial to both sides.

Although after two years the war seems far from over, some social analysts have nevertheless started seriously reflecting upon what has happened insisting there are long term matters that need deeper consideration even at present. In the context of the Russian invasion of Ukraine the obvious has been proclaimed that history that allegedly came to an end has returned. What more does this mean now that history seems to be interfering with the present? As was mentioned in the introduction, in his *The Road to Ukraine* Frank Furedi raises the problem of historical amnesia, the folly of the end of history, and the neglect of the importance of traditional boundaries, both national and cultural, which has had a deleterious effect on the moral preparedness of the West. He continues that as important as rearming the countries of the West may be, "what matters now today is not so much military but moral rearmament." And for this he insists recovering a sense of historical consciousness is the precondition for the Western world to acquire the ability to play "a mature and responsible role in global affairs."[51]

50. Rohac, "Time to Bring Back."
51. Furedi, *Road to Ukraine*, 98.

This valuable advice from Furedi can be just a little easier for many Poles to accept and work upon in their position of a NATO eastern flank country that in the time following the Russian invasion of Ukraine has experienced so much of history—both vicariously and directly. Especially the human element of history that transcends geopolitical matters, as important as these maybe, has been brought home to Poles with tremendous force. And this forwards a more practical kind of "moral rearmament": a measure of moral and social capital seems to have been gained, at least for a time. To give one example, the reaction of Polish authorities to the bomb that landed on the Polish side of the border on November 15, 2022, killing two citizens, was levelheaded and capable of placing the event in the larger context of the massive bombing of Ukrainian civilian targets taking place at the time, even though it remains unclear whether or not it was a case "friendly fire." In other words, consideration of the tremendous tragedy the neighbors were experiencing made a difference. Such a reaction, that included much of Polish society, shows moral growth taking place. The historical context is also obvious, in this and other related events. And that is significant. For as greatly as history has reinstated its influence at this time on Poland and Europe as a whole, both need to be prepared for possibly even greater challenges, of a military nature at worst, but also morally, which may be equally demanding, and for which a broader historical consciousness is among the major prerequisites.

2

Two Empires and the Road to Ukraine

THE FULL-SCALE INVASION OF Ukraine by Russia in February of 2022 demonstrated that an empire like a leopard never seems to change its spots. As most Ukrainians will inform you, the latest invasion is a magnified continuation of the invasion of 2014 when Putin took over Crimea from them: the so called hybrid war that followed was over and open—albeit undeclared—war had begun. Even earlier than either version of war there were the invasions of Chechnya and Georgia. Thousands of refugees from those countries made their way to Poland, of which quite a few passed further on.[1] Chechnya has a much smaller population than Ukraine, but many civilians died in that war and in hindsight it was a harbinger of what is occurring now.

As mentioned earlier, most specifically by Andrew Michta, the war in Ukraine has brought to the fore the question of national sovereignty. Something brought to the fore in this case is something that has been questioned. Most obviously by an aggressive empire against an assailed country, but also less blatantly by what for the time being we will call the liberal empire in relation to its member states. Pierre Manent has persuasively argued: "The sovereign state and representative government are two of the great artifices that have allowed us to accommodate huge masses

---

1. For an analysis of the Chechen refugee waves in Poland, see Pietrasik, *Uchodźcy czeczeńscy*.

of human beings within an order of civilization and liberty." But after the Second World War, he adds, in Europe "the state is less and less sovereign, and government is less and less representative."[2] Manent then goes into a discussion of the relationship of the sovereign nation state in Europe and its relationship with the European Union. In this chapter this problem will also be examined after a closer look at the aggressor and briefly at the assailed nation state, most particularly from the question of its sovereign identify as evidenced by its history.

The Russian empire has a long and bloody history with various guises. In the twentieth century it became incorporated into the Soviet Union: the "evil empire," as Ronald Reagan famously and astutely called it. At its ideological base was Communism, which thanks to Marxism developed what was termed "scientific socialism." Human sacrifices were inconsequential on the road to a glorious future. And sacrifices there were! The authors of *The Black Book of Communism* of 1997 estimated the numbers of victims for all Communist regimes to be around ninety million.[3] The Russian archives of Soviet crimes were only opened for a few years, and so the portion of the above numbers concerning their country's regime of terror are only an estimate, and all the more so in the case of the Chinese, the main perpetrators of the horrendous statistics. It will only be possible to get a more accurate number once Russia and China allow access to their archives, which is virtually impossible in both cases in the foreseeable future. And if what happened in Poland during the transition from Communism to democracy is any indication, much of the contents of those archives will be or already are destroyed.

Decades ago Milan Kundera poignantly noted East Central Europe was made up of "small nations" in light of their tentative existence,[4] and that has now been all too dramatically proved as still true. Putin's attack on Ukraine also brings to mind Stalin's treatment of the country in the infamous Holodomor when millions of Ukrainian peasants starved to death during the brutal collectivization of their land. Now, besides the direct violence to civilians in the modern country, he has destroyed machinery Ukrainians use for sowing and harvesting wheat on their rich land, and initially blocked the Black Sea trade route for the country, so one of the breadbaskets of Europe will be partially unavailable to developing countries, albeit at the

2. Manent, *Democracy Without Nations*, 33.

3. See the discussion of *The Black Book of Communism* in Tismananeanu, *Devil in History*, 30–38, 46–49.

4. Kundera, "Tragedy of Central Europe," 7, 8.

time of writing Ukrainians have alleviated this situation somewhat. This is besides the unimaginable devastation of so much of the infrastructure of their country—both municipal and industrial, among others—the images of which understandably haunt Poles.

In 1985 Joan Baez gave a concert at the Catholic University of Lublin. She had just come from Gdańsk where she had met Lech Walesa, the leader of the banned at the time Solidarity movement. A true entertainer, she demonstrated her sense of the Polish audience with an anecdote of how she had informed a group of young monks that upon leaving Poland she would be meeting with Mark Knopfler of Dire Straits, and upon hearing this "they dropped their rosaries." More seriously, she realized that in Poland of the time there was not much sympathy for movements of the left such as she was identified with. And so she gave the explanation that her true sympathies lie with the downtrodden, for whom it hurts just as much if they are struck by the left hand as the right hand. Unfortunately, the Russian evil empire has demonstrated its ability to strike its victims both with the left hand under Communism, and with the right hand as a national empire at present.

Such deeds are witness to the evil empires are capable of—together with crimes against humanity used as a means to an end—and which the Russian empire with its full-scale invasion of Ukraine demonstrates Europe is no longer free of their effects. At different times as well as from Russia's different imperial incarnations, Poland has been at the receiving end of such actions, some more debilitating—for instance, loss of sovereignty—some less so, where resistance was successful. This is one of the reasons Poles mostly sympathize with their suffering neighbors so, and Polish scholars and thinkers have studied the guilty beast so closely. Among the more recent books is one by a top scholar and historian of ideas, inspired by the invasion of Ukraine but showing its deep roots and national traditions. Andrzej Nowak took the bull by the horns in 2023 in his *Return of the Evil Empire*.

Naturally in the title of his book Nowak is referring to Reagan's use of the term in reference to the Soviet Union mentioned above. More specifically, the American president first used the phrase "evil empire" when he addressed the National Association of Evangelicals on March 8, 1983 at the height of Cold War. It also marked his providential rejection of détente with its ineffectiveness. Nowak's book is actually a collection of essays that he wrote over the years and more recent ones that included analysis of aspects of Putin's invasion. One of his essays analyzes the American strategy toward the USSR over the years and how Reagan effectively modified that strategy, in no small measure through his recognition of the genuine malice of the Communist system. Nowak doesn't recount some of the international responses to the phrase, but for the Polish opposition under the harness of the system it was applauded for the recognition of the genuine nature of the Soviet empire.

With its multiple crimes against humanity—partially even preceding the invasion—and destruction of Ukraine's infrastructure at many different levels, the new imperial Russia is indeed evil, but how does it relate to the Soviet empire? That is an important question if we are to suppose a "return" of the evil empire and not simply a new one. It is certainly a new empire but the relationship to its forerunner can be argued to be also fundamental.

One of the misleading differences is that the imperial robe of Communism was ideologically transnational and the new incarnation is apparently national. Often enough it has been referred to as fascist. But there is a crucial relationship to the two even taking this into account. Inspired to no small extent by Polish philosopher Leszek Kołakowski, Vladimir Tismaneanu has identified the "activities" of the devil—that is, radical evil—through Communism and fascism in the middle of the twentieth century. The latter are more familiar in Western Europe, but Communism's deeds are in many ways even more deleterious. Moreover, for all their differences the two are related in spirit: "Communism and Fascism believed a fundamental change was possible. They engineered radical revolutionary projects in order to answer this belief. However, they enacted their utopias with complete disregard for individual human life. Their frantic acceleration of human history engendered the materialization of radical evil in history."[5]

A diabolical relationship between both forms of tyranny! Symbolic of this is the Molotov Ribbentrop Pact signed by the Nazis and Communists in 1939 that led to their collaboration in starting the Second World War. One might add that in the fatal morning of February 24, the Ukrainian Institute of National Remembrance sent a letter to its partners, informing about the Russian aggression and the beginning of fighting. It also contained the following statement: "We would like to emphasize once again that today's war between the Russian Federation and Ukraine has become possible on a large scale because the crimes of the Soviet communist totalitarian regime have not been properly condemned by the world community. This is clearly seen in the words and actions of the president of the Russian Federation."[6]

5. Tismaneanu, *Devil in History*, 52.
6. Quoted in Kamiński, "Putin Must Be Held Accountable," para. 1.

Łukasz Kamiński argues that obviously the above claim cannot be strictly proven, but many arguments support such a vision of this war's roots. Most importantly, Russia would look different today had that been done: "Such a reckoning would surely have allowed the Russian society to be based on truly democratic values. Condemning lies, dictature and crimes would mean promoting truth, democracy and justice, would make building a civil society possible."[7] Possibly, but not inevitably.

But a major difference between the versions of empire is that the Soviet Union was set on a course of world transformation, which naturally required its dominance of increasing numbers of national communities to achieve, as historical circumstances prominently offered in East Central Europe, whereas Putin's Russia apparently "merely" focuses on regional domination. Of course it does not wish to give up the gains of the Soviet Union—where they remain, like in the unfortunate case of Chechnya—but a varied ideology bolsters its momentum toward further gains. George Weigel notes that Ukraine posed no threat to Russia, "only to its leader's warped ideology."[8]

Ideology is a major factor, if not the only one to consider. But we must also ask what ideology is so potent? Part of Putin's ideology stems from an influential Russian interpretation of history. But this was not just made up in the last moment for the sake of the invasion. It has fairly deep roots. For instance, in *Return of the Evil Empire* Nowak offers the example of a major work that presented an imperial message already at the beginning of this century. In *Russia and the Russians in World History* (2003) Natalia Narochnitskaia—a scholar and deputy of the Duma at the time—wrote a comprehensive history of how Russia defended itself against alleged Western aggression, which included inducing a false sense of nationhood upon the Ukrainians.[9] The Red Army was crucial for the defeat of Nazi Germany, which the author boasts of. Not brought up is that this defeat was necessary only after their erstwhile ally betrayed them. The book concludes with the author's insistence that Russia faces up to the "systemic challenge"—Putin's term—to the country's territorial integrity, and more ominously, as Nowak summarizes the ending of her book: "Russia must defend its great power status in order to rescue its God-given identity and through this—as the

---

7. Kamiński, "Putin Must Be Held Accountable," para. 3.

8. Weigel, "What Ukraine Means," 17.

9. Nowak, *Powrót Imperium Zła*, 393–401.

only country able to resist a wave of global nihilism—save the world."[10] Nowak also points out that Narochnitskaia's perspective on Russian history is illustrative of a certain mindset and far from original. Pundits also point out that Russian thinking was not uniform, severe nationalists, for instance, were critical in that they perceived Putin was rather lax in his imperialism, and were unhappy about this before the full-scale invasion.

Russian ideology accepts a strategy of the ends justifying the means, so disinformation spread to opponents is a key component, sometimes quite effective. Some have claimed Putin's propaganda was more effective than his army. Among them, Mark Galeotti additionally notes, "Putin's agenda of reasserting Russia's status as a great power does not require him to expand its borders . . . , but it does set him against the West. From his point of view, anything that divides, distracts and demoralizes us is useful."[11]

Galeotti makes an exception in this denial of the new empire's need for expansion to its desire to recover what was lost at the end of the Cold War. A good point, but there is more to it than that. One of the key elements in Russia's current aggression toward Ukraine is the ideology of *Russkij mir*— roughly the Russian world. Certainly the interpretation of history—quite close to what was explained above—is one among the tenets of this ideology. What it also implies is the unification of the Russian speaking people of the world, which was among the justifications of the invasion. Not to mention the problem of the growing population of the Muslim speaking republics makes ethnic Russians somewhat nervous, thus increasingly the Slavic population has various motivations.

Putin declared 2007 to be the "Year of the Russian Language." In one of his speeches during a federal assembly that year, he rather benignly but significantly declared:

> This year, the Year of the Russian Language, gives reason once again to remember that Russian is a language of the historical brotherhood of peoples, a language of true international communication. The language is not just the repository of an entire layer of truly world-class achievements, but is also a living space for a multimillion-fold "Russian world," which, of course, is significantly wider than Russia itself.[12]

---

10. See Nowak, *History and Geopolitics*, 261.

11. Galeotti, *Weaponisation of Everything*, 167.

12. Tishkov, "Russian World," 10.

In June 2021 Putin wrote an essay titled "The Historical Unity of Russians and Ukrainians" in which he wrote about the "ethnically Russian people," which included the Russian nation made up of Russians, Belarusians, and Ukrainians. In November 2023, well into the invasion, he reiterates long-standing justifications for the aggression,[13] that is, the "Russian nation" at the center of Russian identity and a wider "Russian world" including other non-East Slavic ethnicities in both modern Russia and the former territory of the Soviet Union and Russian Empire at the ideological heart.

Indeed, until the full-scale invasion, for a large number of Ukrainians Russian was their first language. A report by a Polish war correspondent in the Donbas region provides an incident illustrating how the invasion affected this. Tomasz Grzywaczewski spoke to one of the residents of the region in the early phase of the war: a woman who had a sister in Russia, a not uncommon family situation there. Shortly after the invasion the sister in Russia called her sister in Ukraine asking her how things were going. She would not believe that her sister had to be holed up in an underground bunker because her house had been bombed. The siblings parted ways: one accepting the Russian propaganda for internal use, the other as a Ukrainian patriot, dearly paying the price for that privilege.[14] That provides some idea of why the Russian speakers in Ukraine rejected the Russian world, at least when the war was going well. Veronika Melkozerova, *Politico* Kyiv correspondent, bears witness to that phase. "Russian culture has always served as a façade covering up Russian crimes. But it took two revolutions, a hybrid Russian invasion, an occupation in the east and a full-scale assault for me to understand the connection," she confesses. Melkozerova is critical of those who lag behind, concluding "if anything, we've been too slow in reclaiming our identity from those who tried to erase it."[15]

And so *Russkij mir* is one of the keys to Russian imperialist ideology, and it goes beyond the current ruler. This is one of the points Nowak argues in an interview shortly after the war broke out: what the West must recognize is that "Putin is not the problem. Putin realizes the dreams and aspirations of most of the current Russian elite. In order to turn Russia into a safe partner for its western neighbors, its imperialism, deeply rooted in Russian history and culture, must be stopped."[16]

13. See Bailey et al., *Russian Offensive Campaign Assessment*, 1–2.

14. An exceptional work of war correspondence is Trofimov, *Our Enemies Will Vanish*.

15. Melkozerova, "How I Decolonized," para. 4.

16. Nowak, "Russian Imperial Reconquista," para. 22.

Worth stressing here is also that Ukrainian identity has deep historical roots. In *The Conflict in Ukraine*, written shortly after the initial invasion and occupation of Crimea in 2014, Ukrainian historian Serhy Yekelchyk helps in understanding the actual history of the attacked country. Dalibor Rohac points out that as a consequence of more than four centuries of common history within the Polish-Lithuanian Commonwealth, much of today's Ukraine shares more of its past within that polity than it does with Russia.[17] The historical connection of Ukrainians within the Commonwealth stems from the Lithuanians wresting a number of Ukrainian lands from the Mongol rulers that had occupied Kyivan Rus—which had included Moscow, but that principality remained under Mongol domination till much later. Some Ukrainians refer to the aggressor as Muscovy, considering it a better name for the imperial assailant; similarly, a number of Ukrainian patriotic historians say Russia was actually appropriated from Ukraine, since, as Yekelchyk explains their line or reasoning, "Kyivan Rus, was centered in what is now the current city of Kyiv, while the present day Russian heartland, including the Moscow region, was colonized somewhat later."[18]

When the Grand Duchy of Lithuania united with the Kingdom of Poland, formally in the sixteenth century, the Polish Lithuanian Commonwealth was created, with a form of republican government possessing an elected monarchy. This Polish rule over the Ukrainians was quite different from the imperialist Russian rule to which ever increasing parts of the Ukrainian populace ended up being subjugated to from the late seventeenth century onward, eventually with the result of its culture being banned within the polity. For instance, in the Commonwealth Kyiv was eventually under Magdeburg law, which endowed it with fairly liberal municipal rights. As Yekelchyk writes, "Unlike Muscovy, Poland professed religious tolerance and allowed a significant Jewish population to reside within its borders." Significantly, he continues, "Ukraine's historical relations with Poland and other Western neighbors had a profound and lasting impact."[19] The author mentions the multinational heritage of cities like Lviv as evidence of that. One can add that, in a sense symbolically, Raphael Lemkin, a Polish Jew, studied in interwar Lviv, where he developed the idea of genocide and was one of coauthors of the convention. The Ukrainian lands that remained under the Polish rule and then that of the Habsburg Empire—one of the

17. Rohac, "Time to Bring Back."
18. Yekelchyk, *Conflict in Ukraine*, 26.
19. Yekelchyk, *Conflict in Ukraine*, 26

partitioners of the Polish Lithuanian Commonwealth—received a different exercise of political culture than those under imperialist Russia, together with what we can now call an emergent civil society towards the end of the period, and Ukrainian cultural life flourished.

One more aspect of the Russian world needs examining, especially in light of its progression towards evil. *Russkiy Mir* is an ideology promoted by many in the leadership of the Russian Orthodox Church, ostensibly to save the world from Western "decadence." It may be true, as Lionel Shriver suggests in an opinion piece for *The Spectator*, that with its nihilistic self-absorption "the West plays up to Putin's caricature,"[20] but the Russians have a good deal of difficulty with their own society, where substance abuse, broken marriages and abortions are the order of the day, and one would think the Orthodox Church in the country should primarily deal with these ailments. The major issue in the church's alliance with the evil empire, however, is its breaking the moral rules of just war by accepting a war of aggression, which was even ostentatiously blessed by Kirill, the patriarch of Moscow.

Fortunately, there is resistance to such a blasphemous, Manichean slant to a "religious project." A group of some five hundred Orthodox scholars throughout the Eastern Orthodox world issued "A Declaration on the 'Russian World' Teaching" that was published on March 13, 2022. The declaration begins:

> The Russian invasion of Ukraine on February 24, 2022 is a historic threat to a people of Orthodox Christian tradition. More troubling still for Orthodox believers, the senior hierarchy of the Russian Orthodox Church has refused to acknowledge this invasion, issuing instead vague statements about the necessity for peace in light of "events" and "hostilities" in Ukraine, while emphasizing the fraternal nature of the Ukrainian and Russian peoples as part of "Holy Rus'," blaming the hostilities on the evil "West," and even directing their communities to pray in ways that actively encourage hostility.

Furthermore, the scholars called the Russian world doctrine an "ideology," "a heresy," and "a form of religious fundamentalism" that is "totalitarian in character."[21]

---

20. Shriver, "How the West Plays Up."
21. "Declaration on the 'Russian World,'" 121–22.

By contrast, surveys indicate Ukrainians have become more religious since the invasion. Worth noting in this context, already after 2014 they started working at gaining autocephaly for their Orthodox church, which was granted in 2018, and formally the Ecumenical Patriarch of Constantinople Bartholomew granted a decree of ecclesial independence to the Church in January, 2019. The Orthodox church under Russian jurisdiction still existed in the country, but Orthodox Ukrainians started joining their own autocephalous church in greater numbers after the new invasion, their patriarch acknowledged their necessity for self-defense. While the Ecumenical Patriarch of Constantinople has condemned the invasion.

As Weigel puts it, "By looking death in the eye and refusing to flinch, Ukrainians, both soldiers and civilians, have reminded the West that we are more than our subjectivity." And this gives us an indication of a deeper source of happiness which many seek in vain, and also steers us away from the evil that is close to us: "The secret of happiness is liberty and the secret of liberty is courage, the secret of courage is faith: faith in a larger reality than ourselves; faith in a destiny beyond this life and its great but inevitably transient satisfactions; faith that we are creatures capable of nobility and self-giving, not merely self-assertion and willfulness; faith that solidarity is possible amid plurality; faith that courage can overcome evil, some day."[22] Unfortunately, with the extension of the war over time, the Ukrainians are understandably no longer so fearless and that day where evil is overcome may not be soon, and possibly not at this juncture in time.

The evil empire has indeed returned. And although their burden is the heaviest, it is not only the Ukrainians who must face it. Europeans must start by acknowledging it for what it truly is. But what of the European Union itself? Yoram Hazony argues that after 1989 the EU was an imperialist project "which has progressively relieved member states with many of the powers usually associated with political independence."[23] To what extent is Hazony correct in labeling the polity an empire?

It is true that the EU has been progressively centralized and plans are for this to continue. Marco Duranti has noted "proponents of 'ever greater union' cast the European Union' as more than a technocratic endeavor generating peace through economic integration."[24] What are the

22. Weigel, "What Ukraine Means," 23.

23. Hazony, *Virtue of Nationalism*, 3.

24. Duranti, *Conservative Human Rights Revolution*, 359.

consequences of this in terms of the EU as empire if Hazony is correct in his basic assessment?

It has been suggested by scholars the transnational polity is rather a normative empire.[25] There is also a question of the source of these norms, especially in light of the expansion of the union that allowed for Warsaw–Pact countries to join the special club. As Michael Burleigh puts it, there was a certain undertone to the expansion: "Those used to a familiar Western club were sometimes unenthusiastic about admitting East European states, which Moscow had kept in line, although few were so lacking in taste as to say so openly."[26]

This suspected attitude on the part of the historian gives some idea of the source of the divisions within the predominantly "bureaucratic and legal project"—as he puts it—that will be discussed below. For one thing, the implicit attitude makes it easier to understand the presence of a certain hierarchy in the polity, with the western core at the center.[27] But it also suggests why the rule of law goes beyond democratic governance and can be viewed as one of the instruments of the normative form of imperialism. With this in mind, I will provide a broader introduction to the polity.

There is apparently a fairly common attitude among Eurocrats that a good crisis should not go to waste. And the ideal solution to a crisis is to move toward an "ever closer union," that is to edge the European Union toward a centralized superstate by hook or by crook. One of the major arguments within Stefan Auer's *European Disunion* (2022) is that many of the problems the EU experiences are actually caused by such an elitist current that does not take into account major forces within differing member states.[28]

Auer points out how seductive the European experiment has been both for politicians and scholars of the project with its cosmopolitan supranational goal. This political end has had negative consequences. Technocracy has dominated the supranational project and taken on a life of its own beyond the control of those it was meant to serve. In a manner that is complimentary to Jan Zielonka, where the latter blames the institution's democratic deficit for the populist reaction of a number of national parties, Auer similarly goes on to blame overbearing operations of the Eurocrats,

25. See, for instance, Panke, "EU's Normative Imperialism," 350–63.

26. Burleigh, *Best of Times*, 320.

27. See Zarycki, *Ideologies of Eastness*, 10.

28. Auer, *European Disunion*.

but he does not believe this unseemly response on the part of some member states negates the underlying quest for their national communities' sovereignty within the union. Indeed, he has his criticisms of the concept of "pooled sovereignty" at the base of the EU on the one hand, as well as of Zielonka's notion of Europe as sort of post-modern "neo-medieval empire" on the other.[29]

In essence, the problem according to Auer is the EU's philosophically post-sovereign polity has actually led to the decline of democracy at the national level without enhancing it at the supranational level. This is related to a paradox with deep origins and continuing relevance. He claims Europe is shaped by the ongoing tensions between two tendencies: efforts to maintain the independence of participating member states on the one hand, and the striving for a united, transnational polity on the other. The latter vector was forwarded early on by the first president of the European Commission, Walter Hallstein, for whom what was to become the EU was a transnational project. He was attracted to the functionalist concept of "spillover," which explains the attraction of the politics of the "ever-closer union" that would lead to the empowerment of "supranational institutions at the expense of smaller governing units, including nation states."[30] Hallstein was opposed by French president Charles de Gaulle, an early supporter of the "Europe of nation states," who criticized the commission in 1965 as "a technocracy, for the most part foreign, destined to infringe upon France's democracy."[31] And this struggle, as Auer demonstrates, continues to this day. More recently, former Polish prime minister Mateusz Mazowiecki echoed De Gaulle's complaint.

Nevertheless, the battlefield has evolved. Hallstein was instrumental in transferring the field of struggle more specifically from the Commission to the European Court of Justice (ECJ) through his conception of the "majesty of law." For the integrationist agenda the ECJ evolved as the most powerful body: one that avoids democratic control, it can be added. In 2021 the Polish Constitutional Tribunal questioned the principle of the court's supremacy over the nation's constitution by claiming some of its decisions countered a number of articles in the country's EU accession treaty. Auer notes that this is an old struggle since the German Federal Constitutional Court already did much the same after complaints had been filed against the Maastricht Treaty of 1992. The German court essentially claimed that

29. See Zielonka, *Counter-Revolution.*

30. Auer, *European Disunion,* 14, 15.

31. Quoted in Auer, *European Disunion,* 16.

the European Union "is ultimately derived from democratically constituted member states, which in turn embody the sovereign wills of the peoples of Europe. . . . In sum, the EU is not a state, and should not become one."[32] This decision was criticized at different degrees by a number of pro-integrationist scholars.

Auer argues it is primarily this tension that leads to the growth of populism in Europe. Among other reasons, with the increasing irrelevance of borders he points out—after David Goodhart—the freedom of movement within the union has resulted in the division between the elitist "anywheres" in opposition to the populist "somewheres." People in motion do not concentrate on solving problems in a specific location, such as within the bounds of a national community, and among politicians this division results in policies that lead to dissatisfaction within their electorates. Auer quotes Joseph Weiler: "As Europe after 1989 moved ever further towards a 'political messianic venture *par excellence*,' it compromised its own ability to enhance democratic consolidation in the new member states."[33]

Worth stressing, often noted is the EU establishment has its own problems with democracy, for which the term democratic deficit has become popular among scholars. Perry Anderson describes it as such:

> The EU . . . executives are appointed by governments, not put into office by the votes of citizens; legislative elections yield neither a government nor an opposition; proceedings at every institutional level of the Union, including its judicial and financial arms, are shrouded in secrecy; decisions of the supreme court are immutable. In post-modern style, all this is presented as the last word in an up-to-date polity: in practice, it is the simulacrum of a sentient democracy.[34]

Something similar can be stated regarding the so called European values. In an interview held in 2010 Jacques Delors, former president of the European Commission, speaks of the questions raised in "this Europe of values" in which the shared values are largely hidden on account of an individualism "that is made worse by a world characterized by media coverage and a kind of politics based on public opinion polls. All those values that go to make up a society are being done away with; day after day they

---

32. Auer, *European Disunion*, 43. For a more accessible and developed version of this case, see also Auer and Scicluna, "Poland Has a Point."

33. Auer, *European Disunion*, 34.

34. Anderson, *Ever Closer Union*, 228.

are being destroyed. If the values of Europe are in decline, then it is Europe that suffers."[35]

Significantly, Delors is critical of Eurocrats and politicians who refuse to acknowledge the deeper shared values. For instance, a number of politicians involved in working out the Lisbon Treaty of 2009 refused to have these European axiological roots mentioned. Furedi augments Delors concerns by noting that abandoning tradition in public life is among the reasons for this moral crisis, which we will look at primarily from the perspective of historical memory further on. He adds that, especially among academic circles and the cultural elite, "In Western European public life, arguments and statements that are communicated through a self-consciously moral language are rarely taken seriously in their own terms."[36]

Another problem stemmed from the democratic deficit of the EU governance creating problems with the expansion that speeded up in 2004 when Poland and a number of other former Warsaw Bloc countries joined. As President Jose Barroso informed his audience during the State of the Union conference in May 2013: "We are at a point in time when European integration must be pursued openly, transparently and with the explicit support of the citizens of Europe. The times of European integration by implicit consent of citizens are over. . . . Europe's democratic legitimacy and accountability must keep pace with its increased role and power."[37] In effect he is admitting the problem of democracy in the union without indicating its cause, nor was his warning very effective, as Brexit among others demonstrated.

The "new member states," that is from Central Europe, had their own concerns. For instance, Polish intellectual Marcin Król's warning in the decade following the liberation of the states from Communism, and as the war in Ukraine has more recently brought to the fore once again: "Whoever represents a dualist vision of the world which is dominated either by liberalism, or nationalism is not only wrong about political realities, but causes irreparable damage, because the chances of implementing the liberal democratic project are decreased in direct proportion to the height of the wall between liberalism and nationalism."[38] Over a decade later, when the countries were EU members and Król's warning had not been sufficiently

35. Quoted from Bielefeld and Tietze, "In Search of Europe," para. 3.

36. Furedi, *Populism*, 24.

37. Quoted from Furedi, *Populism*, 22.

38. Quoted from Auer, *European Disunion*, 143.

heeded, Auer defined the nature of the failure further. He argues the country's liberal intelligentsia underestimated nationalism's positive potential and made no attempt to rebuild Polish patriotism, so needed under the new circumstances.

It should be evident the lessons from 1989 were quite different for the Western countries such as Germany and France, and for Central European countries. Ryszard Legutko, Polish author of the philosophical essay *Demon in Democracy: Totalitarian Temptations in Free Societies* (2016), complains about what came to pass went against expectations that innovation was what was expected of them in the new order: "The required attitude of the newly liberated nation was not that of creativity but conformity. . . . The more we copied and imitated, the more we were glad of ourselves. Institutions, education, customs, law, media, language, almost everything became all of a sudden imperfect copies of the originals that were in the line of progress ahead of us."[39]

Auer notes the new member states were accused of "backsliding," among others in questions of rule of law. He adds that the unnoted problem was the rule of law that these countries inherited from Communism was hardly ideal. Thus it is understandable that Janez Janša, a former Slovenian politician, is quite critical of EU governance from such a perspective: "Nothing has significantly changed since the Communist system. The Left is totally dominating the judiciary—the same families as in the past: people who violated human rights, the people who sent us to prison in Communist times. They are still operating in our judicial system. But when we try to make some democratic reforms, we are accused of interfering in the independence of the judiciary."[40]

Is it a wonder at times East Central Europeans feel they are the periphery of the EU empire?[41] Here we can note that it is not only the so called "rule of law" that purportedly aggravates Brussels. Different perspectives on politics as a whole are in practice. One of the feisty Polish pundits responded to criticisms that certain Polish patriotic events seem "fascist." First, in an opinion piece for *Politico* in 2017, Tomasz Wróblewski indicated what should absorb Brussels and Western media more than such events: "Europe is under tremendous pressure from all possible directions. It needs profound market changes and a whole new value system to cope with the

39. Legutko, *Demon in Democracy*, 39, 41.
40. Janša, "Europe Turned away from Democracy," para. 33.
41. See, for instance, Pourchot, "EU's Eastern 'Empire,'" 17–31.

pressure of new cultures and the migration crisis. It also needs to fix the growing rift between North and South and East and West." Thus, he complains labeling some governments as "fascist" does nothing to help solve the problem "especially as those doing so offer no attractive alternatives." Wróblewski concludes, "A few immature extremists don't make Poland a fascist country. What they do instead is reveal how desperate the EU is to use the threat of 'fascists' as an excuse to push for further centralization and bureaucratization."[42]

Similarly, in a column for a British online journal, Fraser Myers pointed out how democracy was quite vibrant in Poland under the rule of the Law and Justice party, with each election gaining higher electoral participation. However, this is not what interested Brussels. When it seemed the party was set to lose power in 2023, from Western European press coverage it became clear:

> In the eyes of the Brussels elite, "democracy" does not mean the free participation of the public, or rule by the majority. It means following the EU's "values" and serving the interests of the Brussels oligarchy. And so parties and politicians that align with Brussels, like [Donald] Tusk and his Civic Platform, are said to represent all that is "democratic" and good. Meanwhile, those that deviate from EU orthodoxies, like Poland's PiS, are cast out as authoritarian threats to the "democratic" order.[43]

What is notable here is that British pundits who have reflected more seriously on what were the causes of Brexit not infrequently look at the problems of Central European countries from a different, often more sympathetic perspective than continental pundits from Western Europe. It has been noted, for instance, particularly the German press has spread negative opinions on politics apparently more concerned with Polish sovereignty, thus earning the labels "'anti-European,' 'populist' and even 'autocratic.'"[44] This in part stems from the poor relations between the countries when the governing parties or coalitions differ so radically in each of the states. This tension continued even in light of the threats either face or perceive in light of the war which results in a fundamentally different view of the war. As an expert quoted in a report for the *Financial Times* puts it: "For the [German] chancellor, what he fears is uncontrolled escalation and the [Russian]

---

42. Wróblewski, "Poland: Patriotic, Not Authoritarian," paras. 8, 15.

43. Myers, "Donald Tusk Is No Friend," para. 9.

44. See Woś, "Poland, Germany and the Fight," paras. 1, 8.

nuclear threat. Whereas to the Polish debate, the threat perception is different: It's about Russian tanks rolling into Warsaw."[45]

One more matter: Western Europe was fairly lax with regards to the Soviet Union during the Cold War. There was even a great deal of sympathy for the Soviet Union, for instance, among top French intellectuals.[46] It would seem this sentiment has a lasting legacy. However absurd it would be to claim an unstated resentment toward Central Europeans exists on account of their role in bringing down the Soviet Empire, there is possibly a grain of truth to the notion.

At this point in exploring an element of the liberation of the Central European countries from the totalitarian past, an additional element might help in comprehending such matters. In his study of so-called civilizational states, Christopher Coker makes the claim that Europe is now a post-Christian civilization.[47] But Coker notes that part of Europe still draws on its Christian heritage and poses the question of whether it is not the case that these usually less liberal countries, as he puts it, of Central Europe do so on account of their experience of Communism. For Marek Cichocki, a Polish political philosopher, the answer to this question is obvious. Through their more than half century experience of the challenge of Communism, Christianity was a beacon of sense to these populations. The experience of truth that accompanied the Christian revelation meant that "a person's freedom and truth of his/her life can never be the product of some ideology or even one political or economic project."[48] And this is a key lesson concerning truth and freedom that the conflict with Communism imparted upon many of the citizens of these nations that was never profoundly experienced by western societies.

In a similar vein Joseph Weiler—an Orthodox Jew himself—even coined the term Christophobia for the negative attitude of European elites toward their Christian heritage, which they did not want to refer to in a potential constitution for the EU in 2005. In an interview given to a Catholic journal in Poland several years later in 2011, he insists that Polish politicians have the responsibility to remind other European politicians of the Christian heritage of the continent, among other things, because he claimed "the European Union cannot be an ethical community if it loses its

45. Quoted in Minder and Pitel, "Poland and Germany," para. 7.
46. See Judt, *Past Imperfect*.
47. Coker, *Rise of the Civilizational State*, 31–38.
48. Cichocki, *Walka o świat*, 160.

memory of what was good and what was bad. A new Europe that has lost its memory cannot be taken seriously."[49] Unfortunately, that memory is on the wane even in the post-Communist countries and at times has difficulty breaking through the fairly common assumption among neophyte post-Christian elites that religion does more harm than good.[50]

Not speaking directly about religion, Borys Gudziak, a Ukrainian Catholic archbishop, puts forth the axiological challenge his countrymen have given to the West. "Ukraine throws down the gauntlet to the dictatorship of relativism, the culture of relativism, a certain culture of narcissism, which is based on everything being connected to 'me,' with 'myself,' my personal chronology." He counters, "people who are prepared to risk their lives, say not 'I' am the beginning and end of everything, something greater exists."[51] Europeans generally have a long way to go to reach that point, but they have great examples so close to them.

Among the reasons Central Europeans sympathized so much with Ukraine after the invasion is because they have suffered so much from "history," and history has remained just below the surface. Symbolic of this in a virtually literal fashion can be the case of the city Lublin in Eastern Poland, where early this century the municipality decided to build an airport. One of the obstacles that had to be overcome was the discovery of a number of World War II mines on the site where airport was to be constructed that the Germans had planted when retreating from the advance of the Red Army. If this remained a problem so many decades later, one can only guess the similar problem that Ukrainians will still have years from now with the horrendous multitude of mines the Russians planted to hinder their attempts to retake their lands.[52]

Similarly, for Frank Furedi, the war in Ukraine confirmed his sense that history had not merely returned, as many commentators insisted, but had never really departed; history entails both continuity and change that must be understood in order to most appropriately respond to events and the world we live in. This is one of the strongest messages of his recent book *The Road to Ukraine*, written while the war still only a few months

---

49. Weiler, "Przedmurze chrześcijaństwa," 28.

50. See Shortt, *Does Religion Do More Harm*.

51. Gudziak, "Ukraiński opór rzuca wyzwanie," 20. The original interview was published in French.

52. Undetected mines will not be the only problem Ukrainians will have to deal with in the coming years: see, for instance, Dettmer, "The Toxic Legacy Putin Is Leaving."

old. Among Furedi's wide ranging interests within his field of sociology and outside of it, likely his best known work concerns the "culture of fear," which we will study in the next chapter. These questions foreshadow issues that are explored at length in the current work.

Furedi visited his native Hungary shortly after the early, drastic stage of the war broke out in February 2022, and he also visited a small village on the Ukrainian side of the border. At the time the conflagration had not yet had any great effect within it but nonetheless many refugees had gathered there. Here he spoke with elder Hungarian villagers there who remembered the various changes of the border in their lifetime. This proved to him how simple people of his country of origin—he left the country with his parents during the revolt of 1956—had a strong historical sense, and further reinforced his conviction that in contrast the Western cultural and power elites had an impoverished historical sense, a virtual "historical amnesia." Much of the book is an exploration of this phenomenon and how it affects the West.

The author notes that when the war broke out, numerous experts and policymakers regarded the renewed invasion as a wake-up call forcing them "to catch up with the realities of a new era." For Furedi, however, "it often seems they [were] not so much catching up with present day realities but very slowly catching up with the past."[53] The author observes that historical amnesia desensitizes people to historical processes that are always with us. Moreover, it is often accompanied by an overbearing sense of the superiority of the present over a past some have referred to as "the bad old days." An ahistorical sensibility was present throughout much of the twentieth century but gained full momentum after the Cold War concluded with the assumption that history had come to an end. To a greater or lesser degree the feeling crossed political divisions. And despite the current crisis the assumption has not been fully disposed of by contemporary power brokers.

Among the symptoms of this failure is the tendency to read the past "backward" without taking into account historical specificity. After the invasion an American trend was to look at the event as an extension of the Cold War: understandably, one might add, considering Putin's earlier reference to the tragedy of the collapse of the Soviet Union. But Furedi places emphasis on the greater geopolitical complexity of these times, which are no longer bipolar, with a greater number of major players in the world. Consequently, he suggests a better analogy is to be found in the complex years leading up to the First World War. "If anything," Furedi

---

53. Furedi, *Road to Ukraine*, 15.

writes, "the situation is even more complicated than in the early part of the 20th century."[54]

And the BRICS meeting in South Africa in August 2023 demonstrated the truth of the author's claim, where the stance toward the war in Ukraine, among other things, was more neutral. Significantly, although they did not invite Putin since on account of his crimes against humanity international law requires that he should be arrested, Russia was nonetheless represented at the meeting. And the expansion of the organization indicated they wished to create an additional center of power. Moreover, Russia is scheduled to host a BRICS meeting.

Part of the complexity stems not only externally from the divisions within the West itself. With the conclusion of the Cold War, the West lost one of the main sources of legitimacy it possessed. According to Furedi the assumed unity that had prevailed succumbed to divisions and cultural conflicts over values. At the bottom of this problem was a greater comprehension of the triumph of the West having been primarily based on the negative contrast with the opponent rather than the ability of providing a positive model of the common good. Unfortunately, this awareness did not lead to overcoming the problem. For similar reasons the post–Cold War malaise also affected the EU, contributing among other things to a technocratic governance blunting democratic procedure. Furedi agrees with those who have identified this crisis with a loss of meaning in the West during this period.

A key factor in the effectiveness of Ukrainian resistance to aggressive Russian imperialism is the willingness of the country's citizens to die for its sovereignty. This is largely incomprehensible in the West where such willingness is largely absent. Furedi persuasively argues that contrary to expert opinion, the diminishing sense of the value of duty, patriotism, altruistic sacrifice, and risk-taking "are underpinned by a sense of cultural disorientation rather than prosperity."[55] He points to the differences in well off European societies, such as in Finland, where 74 percent of citizens surveyed in 2019 indicated they would be willing to fight for their country, as opposed to the Dutch, where a mere 15 percent declared such willingness. In this the Finns are not all that different from the Ukrainians. Furedi indicates a key reason Ukrainians have demonstrated such a fighting spirit is their sense of nationhood having been solidified to a great extent after

54. Furedi, *Road to Ukraine*, 19.
55. Furedi, *Road to Ukraine*, 33.

Russia's earlier attack and seizure of Crimea in 2014. And here a sovereign sense of history is crucial. Furedi cites Ukrainian scholar Giorgij Kasianov, who in an article in *Foreign Affairs* cited earlier stated, "Ukrainians see their existence in time and space as resting on this vision of a sovereign history, emancipated from Russia."[56]

Among the reasons the author notes people in the West have lost this sovereign sense of history stems from the ideology of globalization and how historical memory is treated within it. Besides being a descriptive concept that deals with the internationalization of cultural and economic life, Furedi notes it "has also mutated into an ideology that elevates the status of international institutions and devaluates the role of national governments."[57] For ideologues of globalization, patriotism, and the celebration of local national communities is nonsensical. Cosmopolitanism within a borderless world is the solution. In such circumstances national histories are counterproductive. This has led to an attack on heroes and heroic enterprises, since they are thought of as redundant. This even effects the army in Britain, his homeland, where risk reduction is considered crucial.

One might add that the responsibility for everyone that cosmopolitanism implies leads to responsibility for no one, which also helps explain the lack of willingness to fight for ones neighbors. As Furedi notes, "Many Western supporters of Ukraine stop short of offering genuine and unconditional backing for the right of this nation to exercise its sovereignty. There are frequent calls by the West to 'accept reality in Ukraine.'"[58] Not a great deal has changed since these words have been written, a decline of support could be observed even before the crisis in Israel broke out in October 2023.

This attitude has some commonality with the depreciation of the nation that accompanied the establishment of the European Union. West German chancellor Konrad Adenauer felt doing away with nation states would make war impossible in Europe. As he put it, "If the idea of European community should survive for fifty years, there will never again be a European war." But, as Hazony points out in response to this claim, the overwhelming evil of Nazi-era Germany did not stem from its being a nation, since the German-speaking peoples did not constitute a nation, which is why historically, he argues, "Western Europeans had not feared

56. Kasianov, "War over Ukrainian Identity," para. 20.
57. Furedi, *Road to Ukraine*, 4.
58. Furedi, *Road to Ukraine*, 54.

Germans because of their nationalism, but because of their universalism and imperialism."[59]

One of the current sources of misunderstanding the past is a sense of presentism that affects politicians as well as others within the cultural elite.[60] This absence of a sense of the past leads to errors by policymakers. The understanding behind presentism is that often even relatively recent events "are confined to a folder in the archives marked the past." Furedi notes how right up to the last moment "so many commentators concluded that Russia's invasion of Ukraine in 2014 did not necessarily serve as a precedent for conflict in the future."[61] Worth adding is that commentators are one thing, but as mentioned earlier European politicians intensifying commercial relations after that invasion and thus partially financing the current one is another. Moreover, in Western Europe what Furedi terms a Year Zero historical policy is forwarded based on the bestiality of its history during World War II. This also leads to a selective approach by the EU to the history of its newer members.[62] For instance, in the House of European History in Brussels, opened in 2017, which Furedi points to as an instrument of Year Zero historical policy, post–World War II events in Central Europe like the Soviet invasion of Hungary in 1956 that forced the author's family to flee their country or the similar invasion of Czechoslovakia in 1968 were left out.[63] But such events help explain why there is a stronger sense of sovereign history in Central Europe that is incomprehensible and even denigrated by the major power players in Brussels and much of Western Europe.

What is interesting in the case of the House of European History is how one of the incidents occurring when it opened in 2017 offers an example of how Eurocrats see Poland. Polish reporter Anna Słojewska published a report in *Rzeczpospolita* where she stresses the fact that the museum's exhibition presents a highly western European perspective. This is striking when it comes to the Cold War. In the exhibition there is not much difference between the opposing super powers, with a number of equivalences; for instance, the Warsaw Pact was simply a response to NATO, etc. As the author indicates, "This strange symmetry is not accompanied by any commentary,

59. Hazony, *Virtue of Nationalism*, 41.

60. The cultural elites Furedi describes are similar to the meritocracy of Sandel's study *Tyranny of Merit*.

61. Furedi, *Road to Ukraine*, 61.

62. See Furedi, *Populism*, chapter 4.

63. See Garbowski, "Polish Debate," 60–70.

such as the fact that on the one side there were democratic countries, on the other countries occupied by the Soviet Union."[64] Słojewska adds that the German perspective is evident in the presentation of 1989, where the breaking of the Berlin Wall is given precedence in the fall of Communism, with no mention of the role of Ronald Reagan and John Paul II.

A month later the same newspaper published a critique of Słojewska's review written by Jaume Duch Guillot, the press secretary of the European Parliament, among other things accusing the journalist of not having studied the exhibition carefully enough. The journalist was naturally quite surprised by this turn. After having revisited the exhibition and verifying her first impressions, she starts her point by point rebuttal of the critique with the statement:

> I read the letter of the European Parliament concerning my article on the House of European History with astonishment. I naively thought it is a place for reflection upon the history of our continent, in which each of us can perceive the history differently. That is not so. As it turns out, my piece "does not present the content of the exhibition in the correct manner" [she quotes the press secretary]. And that is why the parliament, in other words the EU administration, writes the correct interpretation.[65]

When Słojewska comes to the point the press secretary made about her "incorrect" evaluation of the presentation of the Holocaust, she retorts that she continues to claim that it was a threadbare presentation. She adds, "This curious omission was the subject of an article published by the Belgian daily *Le Soir*, with the telling title: 'The House of European History: the museum, which is missing a *GREAT* detail.' I know that in the case of this report the European Parliament did not send a critique. Does that mean that a Belgian journalist has the right to his opinion, but a Polish one does not?"

Presentism degrades the past and promotes idiosyncratic values in the present. Furedi points out that in the British State, institutions ignore historically significant ideals that made it possible to defend the state in the past. Thus the Ministry of Defence has "fallen prey to the fashionable fads associated with identity politics." By the time of the current Russian invasion of Ukraine even British soldiers were engaged in campaigns in this vein. "Confronted with the infantilised behaviour of these soldiers,"

---

64. Słojewska, "Co najbardziej grozi Europie," A11.
65. Słojewska and Guillot, "Jak mamy myśleć," 7.

Furedi concludes, "one is reminded of [the] warning [issued] by the Roman philosopher Cicero when he stated, 'to remain ignorant of history is to remain forever a child.'"[66]

Among the important features of a national community is the nature of relationships it creates within its citizens. To give some idea of the nature of these it is worth looking at the problem of trust within the nation, which cannot be developed without internal relationships at the personal and institutional levels. In *Trust: A History* (2014), Geoffrey Hosking has indicated that the basic unit of trust in a community is the family: from it the rings of trust expand outwards to largely end at the evolving nations. Hosking looks at the European Union and its modestly successful attempts at providing "a broader radius of trust" for its older and newer members, but points out that when a crisis breaks out, the peoples of the various national communities look to their own nation-states for solutions and protection, a point now made all the more evident by Ukraine's response to Russian aggression. Hosking adds that with all its resources more finely attuned to its citizens' needs, the nation state will probably "outbid all rivals in providing a focus for different kinds of trust for the foreseeable future."[67] Trust is thus an element of creating a larger community conducive to the common good at a fundamental level, but it can only be spread out so far while remaining a relevant social force. Which is why it is troubling that globalization ideologues have no understanding for the resurgence of the nation state on a number of fronts. Including, as is now obvious, in the question of security and defense.

At this point it is worth returning to that sovereign history once again which plays such a role in Ukrainian resistance to aggressive Russian imperialism. The Ukrainians were largely unprepared for the first Russian invasion, but in response they rapidly prepared themselves for the present war since they knew the long lasting imperialist inclinations of their aggressor. Crucially, they also had a good sense of who they were despite the complications of their history. This is evident in Yekelchyk's book, presented earlier, which is written to explain the plight of the Ukrainians and also to communicate the knowledge of the Ukrainian's sovereign sense of history to people of the West who did not have a good idea about what had just happened in his country. What we have in a substantial part of

66. Furedi, *Road to Ukraine*, 70.

67. Hosking, *Trust: A History*, 194.

the work is identity history in a national perspective.[68] Yekelchyk also gives a clear picture of contemporary Russian identity, from a top down perspective dictated by Putin. "The ideology of the Putin regime is devoid of communist elements," he notes, "but it valorizes Russia's past as a great power, be it in tsarist or Soviet times. It is the loss of great-power status and empire that explains the Putin regime's negative view of the Soviet Union's dissolution."[69] And this also explains Russia's attitude to the West and the sense of Ukraine as a battleground between them, an explanation that has gained even greater validity.

At the time *The Conflict in Ukraine* was written in 2015, significant divisions still existed within Ukraine among other things reflecting its twentieth century history which the author explains, divisions that as a result of the most recent phase of aggression have been greatly mollified. In the interwar period, although Ukraine announced its independence in 1918, actually both in the lands of the former Habsburg and Russian empires, the part of their lands that was not taken over by the Soviet Union was divided among Poland, Hungary, Romania, and Czechoslovakia. Ukraine was "united" under Soviet rule after World War II, but subject to indoctrination and "fraternal relations" with Russia. A Polish reader of the book will recognize the ironic connotations of such phrases, demonstrating Orwellian newspeak. And even in the interwar period, despite the creation of their own Soviet republic, during the collectivization of farmland Ukrainians experienced the Holodomor, where millions of them died. Ukrainians were not alone in suffering the deadly effects of this phase of Stalinization, but it is estimated approximately half the deaths were theirs despite the considerably smaller portion of the Ukrainian population in the USSR at the time.

Ukrainian history becomes more complicated during the Second World War and Yekelchyk is not afraid to deal with dark cards from that period, noting that Putin has used this in an exaggerated fashion in his historical propaganda regarding the Ukrainian EuroMaidan activists. The same is true of the autocrat's use of history in the current phase of the war. Needless to say, since Ukraine was not included in the expansion of the EU to post-Communist countries, its path since finally gaining its independence in 1991 has been even more difficult than that of such countries as Poland. All in all the author ably explains a complicated history and present, the latter now also a part of its and our history. Yekelchyk concludes

68. For an explanation of identity history, see Bloxham, *Why History?*

69. Yekelchyk, *Conflict in Ukraine*, 8.

with an evaluation of the earlier stage of the conflict that from today's perspective seems prophetic: "Viewed from a longer historical perspective, it is clear that the crisis in Ukraine is only masquerading as ethnic strife. It is a conflict over what type of a state and society will develop in the post-Soviet political space, and a part of Putin's challenge to the unipolar world order that emerged after the Cold War."[70]

This battle for different political orders, which has advanced considerably since Yekelchyk published his book, is also one in which the manner of civilization will prevail is likewise crucial. As Zelensky informed Anne Applebaum and Jeffrey Goldberg when they met him in Kyiv in the spring of 2023, this is a war over a fundamental definition of not just democracy but civilization, a battle "to show everybody else, including Russia, to respect sovereignty, human rights, territorial integrity; and to respect people, not to kill people, not to rape women, not to kill animals, not to take that which is not yours."[71]

Among the more obvious lessons of the current war is that at present soft power in itself is not enough. The overreliance on this nature of force together with mere economic leverage is also among the factors that led to a security crisis in Europe that the closer the country is to the Ukrainian border—not to mention the Russian border—the more intensely it is felt, making rearmament one of the key solutions. However, in his conclusions Furedi raises the following additional matter of the "moral disarmament of the West," which as we have mentioned earlier raises the problem "moral rearmament"; consequently, and worth reiterating, the recovery of a sense of historical consciousness "is the precondition for the Western world to acquire the ability to play a mature and responsible role in global affairs."[72] What is evident is that the moral rearmament he recommends is not the same as soft power, since it does not deny the need for hard power, but puts it in proper perspective. Nevertheless, the paradox in Europe with its EU technocrats seems to be that moral rearmament is also a necessary prerequisite to fully understand the need of a military rearmament at more than a superficial level. And not just for itself and the security of its members, but for also for the sake of Ukraine, since even victory now, if it occurs, will not necessarily bring a lasting peace. History will doubtlessly continue even

70. Yekelchyk, *Conflict in Ukraine*, 161.

71. Applebaum and Goldberg, "Counteroffensive," 20–21.

72. Furedi, *Road to Ukraine*, 92, 98.

under the most optimistic of potential circumstances—which currently seem not so likely.

Auer's book was published shortly after the Russian full-scale invasion of Ukraine, so it was effectively written and edited before the event. Fortunately for the current reader, an author's note, placed after the conclusion, was added pertaining to the invasion, which he states was hardly surprising as such for experts, except for its scale. What is noteworthy, the book contains a chapter on the earlier return of geopolitics, in which the preliminary invasion and occupation of Crimea in 2014 is dealt with in depth, and that takes on an added weight as a result of the later one. Auer points out that while the European Union did participate in some of the events preceding that first Russian aggression as a normative power, he argues its essentially apolitical approach backfired, "triggering bloody conflict and unwittingly encouraging Russia's neo-imperial ambitions."[73]

In the pithy author's note, written a month after the outbreak of the radically more aggressive new phase of the war, Auer expresses his surprise at the apparent unity and speed with which the EU now responded. Especially since there was a mixed response before its outbreak. Most notably France and Germany felt European security was dependent on maintaining relations with Russia, not to mention the horrendous German reliance on Russian gas. Worth adding here, John Lough goes deeply into the latter country's "Russian problem," among other things showing the malady's profound historical roots.[74] Fortunately German support did eventually grow in 2023, with the country becoming a major contributor. Auer likewise wonders whether EU institutions "can afford ongoing confrontation with Poland over its judicial reforms at the same time as Poland is playing a leading role in assisting its neighbor's fight for survival."[75] He also questions how long this sense of unity can last. That is indeed a seminal question, considering, among other matters, the EU institutions did not given up their bullying of Poland during the rule of the Law and Justice party despite the war. Some pundits claim in the national election in 2023 actions of the Eurocrats aided the opposition to the ruling party that Brussels did not like.

Among the reasons for this, besides the question of the rule of law, which will be dealt with later, as mentioned earlier there was the problem of "European values." This has different levels depending on the political

73. Auer, *European Disunion*, 109.

74. Lough, *Germany's Russia Problem*.

75. Auer, *European Disunion*, 187.

reality they address. In 2017 French president François Hollande blithely informed the new EU members states from Central and Eastern Europe: "You have your principles, we have structural funds."[76] The "we" standing for the countries of the so-called Old Europe. Wojciech Roszkowski recalled these words at the beginning of the Russian invasion of Ukraine, and pessimistically noted: "A lot had to change for things to remain the same. The providers of huge funds feeding Putin's war machine still lecture Poland on the rule of law and pretend to see no difference between the defence against the migrants invading the EU from Belarus and the help offered to Ukrainian refugees."[77]

Burleigh also indicates what was noted earlier: "Populism suggests something has gone very wrong with the elites."[78] The problem with the elites in some ways is more pronounced after the war began, or at least poses a greater problem. The EU elites, Eurocrats, can predominantly be called "anti-populists." The populists are often enough found in East Central Europe, although at the time of writing they are spreading. In his book *Populism and the European Culture Wars*, Furedi notes the paternalistic view of the EU towards East Central Europe and the double standard that is applied to the allegedly more politically backward part of the extended union. For instance Hungary was reprimanded when it built a fence to keep out immigrants after the crisis of 2015, but Norway, which took the same action for the same purpose, was virtually ignored. Nevertheless the greatest hypocrisy in Furedi's view is when the "anti-populists" act in an intolerant manner toward the "populists" and remain blind to their own illiberalism. The author feels the term populist is a misnomer in some instances, but maintains it to highlight the faults in the anti-populist stance regardless of how their opponents can actually be evaluated.

Different sets of values, Furedi claims, would not be the source of such difficulties if genuine channels of communication existed. However, the anti-populists hurl calumnies at those who differ in their visions of how the EU can be organized and what values it should support, labeling the populists, among other things, as Eurosceptics with whom no genuine discussion is possible or necessary. "There is no dialogue between the anti-populist and the populist," the scholar claims, "which is why the current

---

76. Quoted in Roszkowski, "What Happened to European Values?," para. 1.

77. Roszkowski, "What Happened to European Values?," para. 6.

78. Burleigh, *Best of Times*, 353.

polarization between the antithetical values is so dangerous."[79] Furedi sees greater danger from the post-nationalist anti-populists who steer dangerously close to denying the validity of representative democracy. Conversely, he asserts, "The experience of history indicates that popular sovereignty and the values associated with its exercise is the most robust foundation on which public life can flourish."[80]

But another aspect of this axiological division is that it also is present within the national communities and this gives those who are more in line with the Eurocrats—in this case the meritocracy—considerable influence with the latter even when they are not in power. Moreover, this imitation that Legutko complained of was hardly necessary for the Communist elite who fed upon the pro-Communist sympathies in Western Europe, since "following some slight touch-ups and finding themselves in new circumstances, the former members of the Communist Party adapted themselves perfectly to liberal democracy. . . . Soon they even joined the ranks of the new guardians of the new orthodoxy."[81] This is hardly surprising, since it fits with what has been brought to light above.

Hazony argues that nations obviously have their faults, nevertheless "liberal imperialist political ideals have become among the most powerful agents fomenting intolerance and hate in the Western world today."[82] This insight brings us to another question more or less along the lines of Eurocrats taking advantage of a crisis, connected with the question of the potential further expansion. It is obvious that despite its flaws, joining the EU would be very positive for Ukraine. As Carl Bildt puts it, "For Ukraine, joining the EU is more than just a matter of stability. It is also a matter of future prosperity."[83] However, the Germans and French wish to take advantage of new members—Moldavia, among others, also comes into play—and enforce changes in the politics of the union, ostensibly to make it easier to govern. While that may be true to some extent—it only takes one Orban to limit economic support for Ukraine in desperate times—it would also make it easier for the power brokers, i.e., the major players, to achieve many of their own ends. And virtually all vestiges of national sovereignty would

79. Furedi, *Populism*, 122.

80. Furedi, *Populism*, 129.

81. Legutko, *Demon in Democracy*, 2.

82. Hazony, *Virtue of Nationalism*, 11.

83. Bildt, "Promise and Peril," para. 24.

be lost for member states, except the most powerful. Thus the democratic deficit would increase, and subsidiarity dispensed with.

Introduced in the Lisbon Treaty, the principle subsidiarity was supposed to assist in the relationship between the national members and Brussels by limiting the infringement of the latter in national politics. As Dalibor Rohac explains, "In simple terms, a group of national parliaments can raise reasoned objections to a legislative proposal in the early stages of the legislative procedure . . . if they believe that the law infringes on the idea of subsidiarity and unduly encroaches on the sovereignty of member states."[84] After this, the proper authority is to examine the problem. Not a very effective defense of national sovereignty, but without it such matters would be worse. And the signs for its further survival are not very positive. For instance, among recent reforms the possibility of vetoing certain EU parliamentary measures, for instance in foreign policy—a domain of nation states—has been suggested. The EU would thus be governed top down, with member states possessing less powers of self-governance than American states in the country's federal system: in a word, the union would be transformed into a superstate.

Moreover, despite German promises to increase spending on a military buildup, although they are slowly being implemented, for a considerable time there had been little substantive improvement.[85] Auer concludes his book with a stirring, extremely pertinent wake-up call:

> The return of war to Europe will further intensify the contest between technocratic "rule of rules" and the "politics of emergency," both of which have eroded democracy in Europe and reduced the ability of its sovereign nations to act. Whether Europe's post-heroical and post-political societies will prove capable of overcoming their limitations will impact decisively not only on the future of Ukraine and Russia, but on the Western world as we know it. A rules-based international order can only be restored when democratic nations prove able and willing to fight for it. Is this asking too much?[86]

And so are the "democratic nations" of Western Europe ready to fight for democracy in their nearest vicinity? A half a year after the Russian invasion of Ukraine, reporters from *Politico* echoed Michael Fallon's opinion

---

84. Rohac, *Towards an Imperfect Union*, 171.

85. See Karnitschnig, "Truth about Germany's Defense Policy."

86. Auer, *European Disunion*, 194.

when they noted that despite the rhetoric with regards to Putin's "genocidal onslaught against the biggest country entirely within Europe, France and Germany spent seven months relying militarily on Washington, and to a lesser extent on Britain, to guarantee democracy and freedom in a close EU ally."[87] Furthermore, this was obviously a matter of political will on their part, not the countries' financial resources. Almost a year later after the Vilnius NATO summit of July 2023, Andrew Michta notes that some very important regional plans were made; however, the key challenge facing the allies would not so much entail adopting the plans themselves as much as they confront the needs for the members' security. Rather, he insists "the most urgent question that will be posed at the summit will be how the allied governments react to those capabilities' targets, i.e., whether they will be willing to properly resource their militaries and, simply speaking, rearm." On account of the post-Cold War "peace dividend" that allowed the countries decades of neglect in the sphere, he adds:

> Europe has so thoroughly disarmed that by my estimates it will take about a decade to bring back the requisite capabilities the alliance needs. . . . For the necessary changes to take place, allied governments will have to take tough political decisions to spend real money on defense. That is why what will happen after the Vilnius summit will arguably be more transformative for the future of NATO than the declarations and the communiques issued during the meeting itself.[88]

Michta rightly stresses the lagging of the NATO members in coming to terms with—primarily—Europe's security needs. But there is another aspect of the war in Ukraine and the West's response that should be taken into account. As analyst at the Stockholm Centre for Eastern European Studies at the Swedish Institute of International Affairs Andreas Umland stresses, "With its ruthlessness, Russia has diminished the stability of the European security order, the coherence of the international order, and the power of the Western community of states. And the longer the war lasts, the larger the damage will be."[89] And he blames Western countries for their lackluster support of Ukraine and lack of will to bring Russia to justice and pay for its crimes.

87. Caulcutt et al., "When Will Europe Learn," para. 5.
88. Michta, "What Happens after Vilnius," para. 3.
89. Umland, "Russia Must Be Held," para. 19.

One can add that with the conflict between Armenia and Azerbaijan in Nagorno-Karabakh, forcing around one hundred thousand ethnic Armenians living in the breakaway region into exile, as well as the Hamas attack on Israel—all within a couple of months of each other in 2023—it seems violent solutions to political issues are becoming something of a horrendous trend.[90] Cichocki argues these developments are ominous harbingers of a new world order, where "instead of creating a world of cooperation and free exchange between states and nations, we are returning to a reality, in which smaller nations and states are becoming pawns in the play of aggressive powers."[91]

Not to mention they have exposed further weaknesses of the European Union, such as the migrant policy has meant the rise of radical Islam, with some terrorism, and a great deal of anti-Semitism in a number of its member states. This is especially disconcerting in Germany, given its history. Among further negative signs is the slow decline and relative chaos of the EU. The German economy, which for years now has been the driving force of the polity, is currently stagnant—the country has even been symbolically labeled "the sick man of Europe" in major news venues. This has had dire political consequences within the country, for instance with the rise of radical parties that can no longer be ignored. Similarly in France the center has been eroded, and after Macron's last term in office expires it seems a right-wing president will reign next, and that is not the only political force in the country that is negatively inclined toward the EU. It has been suggested the union will not likely be abandoned, but sabotaged to an extent that makes it largely unworkable, even in comparison to the problems it currently experiences.

Not a few of these problems that bode for terrible economic consequences are the result of the lack of innovation within the countries, partly dragged down by overregulation. A Polish participant in EU committees devoted to developing policies for enterprise in the polity reported that regulations often stultify initiatives through virtue-signaling. Federalization, ergo centralization, it has been pointed out by experts, will hardly resemble the historic process of the United States, where larger states do not impose their will on smaller ones, thus it will not help if the common market is

---

90. Although the conflict between Armenia and Azerbaijan in Nagorno-Karabakh has received the least attention, it may indicate cracks in the Russian empire. See Kaplan, "Cost of Russia's Collapsing Empire."

91. Cichocki, "Zaklęcia Brukseli już nie działają," 4.

not increased; originally it was a factor in creating wealth and stimulating the entrepreneurial spirit in the European community, but it has not been extended to the service sector of the economy which now dominates in the EU. That is only one of the problems.

All this at a time when the world order is changing. Gabriel Elefteriu rings a strong warning bell. The world order is changing with an ever increasing number of crises and Europe needs to change its priorities. Security is a major issue and Ukraine must be supported, as Russia senses the EU's weakness. He insists how the state works must be reconceptualized: "Across the West and Europe especially, we need to somehow build this into the concept of *resilience*. We need a responsive State, and we need buffers or Reserves, to call upon quickly in order to contain crises."[92]

And so Auer's question is becoming more urgent, but the response from Brussels remains to be seen. The above does not bode well for the long term effort of the European Union to spend more on the necessary means to guarantee the security of its most exposed members. If Auer claims the EU limits democracy in the nation-states—which seems to be an ever increasing problem—the normative empire certainly has its own weaknesses.

Needless to add one of the negative factors generating this state is the European Union's failure to even recognize these problems. Moreover, the war in Ukraine makes evident the EU should also take upon itself a moral rearmament, starting with a renewed recognition of the civilization at its base together with its moral and religious heritage. But within an amorphous technocratic polity that can hardly be imagined as ever taking place, however much it is needed.

92. Elefteriu, "Post-Ukraine, Everything Has Changed," para. 25.

3

The National Community, the Common Good, Historical Memory, and Moral Rearmament

C. C. PECKNOLD DISCERNS A restlessness in democracies paralleling Augustine's insight that we are pilgrims who can only find rest in God.[1] The question arises, in the sea of time, where can we find a ship that allows a political community to float rather than sink in its journey, both in its secular and transcendent course?

The sense of pilgrimage came very early for Poles. Dariusz Karłowicz and Marek Cichocki argue it can be determined from the nation's first leader accepting baptism at the end of the tenth century. From the beginning, Poland's fate gained the element of eschatological hope that added the transcendental point of reference: "And so in the Polish case politics in the communitarian dimension gained a totally exceptional character of a pilgrimage, from which it is not possible to reduce to any flat, materialistic dimension of history."[2] And thus the national community was in a sense born. From there the question of the common good for that special political community arises, and one of the supportive elements is found in a shared historical memory, especially in times of trial.

1. Pecknold, *Christianity and Politics*, 140–41.
2. Cichocki and Karłowicz, "Galeria Polaków," 8.

Turning points in history bring this restlessness in democracies to the fore on a number of fronts. Stefan Auer essentially asks in the previous chapter whether in light of the transformed world order that the Russian invasion exposed Western democracies to, can they fight to defend their values? A crucial question in light of this is whether they can overcome fear, which is an ongoing struggle. In his book *How Fear Works* (2019), Frank Furedi makes the claim a culture of fear in the West that includes various forms of competitive scaremongering marks this century. He persuasively insists, "Paradoxically, the contestation of moral authority, and the weakening of the moral consensus of what to fear, intensify the tendency to moralize threat."[3] And this has a considerable effect on how the past is interpreted: "The mentality it cultivates is one that regards the past as a scary and ignoble succession of events, where humanity lacks not only direction but any redeemable qualities."[4] And so, "The shift of focus from the historical hero to the survivor of history mirrors the trend towards the emergence of the fragile and vulnerable subject as the central character in the culture of fear."[5]

Put simply, for national communities in Europe, since history has brutally returned—with potentially further victims for those closest to the line of fire—so has the need for heroes. The historical amnesia, which Furedi has diagnosed, inhibits the necessary moral rearmament needed to face the challenges the war in Ukraine has evoked. One would think of all places in Europe where this would not be a great problem would be in Poland, since awareness of history has played such an important role in creating the modern national character and—one might add after Robert D. Kaplan—developing a tragic sense to aid in dealing with current mounting dangers. And as we have seen this is true to an extent, especially in the early phases. But it does seem despite this the Polish meritocracy, like its historically less tried European counterparts, similarly implicitly wishes to live up to Michael Sandel's claim that the common good is not among its major concerns.

Let's start with little bit of history to eliminate amnesia with regards to a Polish crisis that preceded the war in Ukraine. In 1241 one of the armies of the Mongol Golden Horde cut a devastating path across Poland, and among others in some battles used human shields. Among these were

3. Furedi, *How Fear Works*, 119.
4. Furedi, *How Fear Works*, 238–39.
5. Furedi, *How Fear Works*, 239.

captured children. Over the ages, as Chantal Delsol notes, that method has been repeatedly used: "Women and children have been placed before attacking armies, to weaken an opponent through a feeling of moral fault. It can't be called anything other than barbarism."[6] Currently, using civilian human shields by an aggressor is considered a war crime. But this does not stop terrorists from their horrendous use. A prime example has been Hamas in its recurrent attacks of the Israeli state over the decades, culminating with the war it initiated in 2023.[7] These uses of human shields are inordinately difficult to deal with and often the defender is faced with such despicable aggressive acts that through the necessary responses unfortunately the innocent become victims, and thus the defender gains an air of odium from those who don't understand what is actually going on.

In 2021 Putin's vassal Lukashenko forwarded a multitude of refugees primarily from the Middle East across his border with Poland. At that time disoriented people could be uncertain of the nature of the crisis. Delsol, however, accurately assessed the situation Poles were faced with: "There is no good 'solution,' it's primarily a case of a tragic situation. It's necessary to demonstrate realism and not give in to blackmail. There is no other possible response."[8]

But after the invasion of Ukraine the following year it was obvious this was a hybrid war effort steered by Putin and these weaponized refugees can effectively be called human shields. "The attack was thwarted," as Tomasz Wróblewski notes, "thanks to the government's determination and overwhelming public pressure."[9] Another commentator further suggests Poland was supposed to be paralyzed by the influx of refugees in order to be hampered in its efforts to help Ukrainians after the already planned invasion. If the Polish authorities had succumbed fully to humanitarian demands—a good number of refugees that undertook accepted venues were accepted—during that invasion tens of thousands of refugees present in the country would attempt to break through the German border without visas, a typical strategy, thus creating far greater chaos than was the case after the war started, and Poland would have been unable to help Ukrainian refugees to the extent that it did. Even at this point, since there are still a significant number of non-Ukrainian refugees entering the country, most of whom

6. Delsol, "Polska w obliczu szantażu," 1.

7. Kamman, "Hamas Positioned Rockets."

8. Delsol, "Polska w obliczu szantażu," 1.

9. Wróblewski, "Poland Heads to the Polls," para. 6.

attempt to pass on to Germany, the German authorities are quite upset, thus the point the commentator made was a valid one. And so, if true the aim did not succeed, yet an odium was nevertheless internationally attached to the attacked Poles. Not to mention a number of the "refugees" literally attacked the border guards. Some of the more aggressive migrants were Kurds. It is known that Putin supports the Kurds in the Middle East.[10] This provides further evidence how the dictator feeds on human misfortune.

Kaplan writes in *Tragic Mind* (2023) that the burden of power is overwhelming.[11] Such is the case of what the border guards had imposed upon them by the horrendous task they were confronted with. Kaplan goes on to note that often intellectuals and journalists do not understand the difficult decisions that must be made and thus pronounce judgment upon authorities without these considerations. This is to no small extent the case with Polish artists such as Agnieszka Holland and her film *Green Line* of 2023.

Obviously an artist has the right to his or her opinions—and sensitivities, some quite laudable, others less so. And there is a degree of complexity to the work above in the case of Holland. But there is also the question of the times. Furedi convincingly argues the West's concentration on the antihero and victim has robbed it of the ability to defend itself. We noted earlier he cites a statistic from a survey that only fifteen percent of the Dutch are willing to defend their country—not unusual in Europe. After the Polish cultural meritocracy largely submitted to the culture of fear in Furedi's sense, possibly the last major film to positively present a hero in Polish cinema was Andrzej Wajda's *Wałęsa: Man of Hope* (2013).

But most European countries are not eastern flank NATO countries like Poland happens to be. Things are not going particularly well for Ukraine and—although as tough as things are going for the at the time of writing Ukrainians nonetheless reject such an option—even a negotiated peace seems somewhat optimistic. As mentioned earlier, even if Putin accepted such a treaty in all likelihood such an outcome would be a mere ceasefire.[12] And that means there is some possibility that one of these flank countries—Poland among the foremost—might at some point in time face its own similar trial. The country is obviously arming itself but heroes would also be needed. For better or worse, with its historical politics and other means during the time of its rule, the "populist" government tried to

10. See Burleigh, *Best of Times*, 185–90.

11. Kaplan, *Tragic Mind*, 77–84.

12. See, e.g., Giles, "Russian Defeat Is More Dangerous," 26–27.

get this message across to Poles. It would be laudable if artists with their talents—and influence—could help rather than hinder in this arduous labor of overcoming a culture of fear.

Heroes mostly emerge from communities where the common good is a genuine concern. Among the difficulties of creating the common good in contemporary, largely consumerist societies is the self-centered individualism they tend to foster. Individualism does not necessarily go along with being self-centered, but the pairing is nevertheless common enough to not rarely affect substantial segments of societies. At one of its seeming societal high points in the final decades of the last century the phenomenon was labeled a "culture of narcissism." The prominent communitarian philosopher Charles Taylor challenged that charge by forwarding an interpretation that members of these developed societies were primarily bound by an ethics of authenticity wherein they aspire to be true to themselves and their originality. He also proffered some ideas as to how the ethos can avoid being trivialized and better serve society. In *The Disappearance of Rituals* of 2020 Byung-Chuk Han cites but is not convinced by these arguments. In contrast to Taylor's claims he curtly states, "The narcissism of authenticity undermines community."[13] Han objects to the alleged moral facade of contemporary authenticity, claiming it leads to a form of self-exploitation, which the neoliberal regime appropriates into its production process. The seeming originality of individuals is actually a form of conformism. A Polish anthropologist looks at the narcissistic conformism evidenced in a common trend of the current digital era in the country. According to Roch Sulima:

> The philosophy of a selfie is nothing other than a cheap, fleeting attempt at self-definition. Earlier there was the category of personality. This was something fashioned through the dynamics of relationships with others, it is not defined through genetics. A sense of the self resulted from where we belonged, we are with these ones or with others. Now, when in each moment we can be with the whole world, this has faded. . . . This forces upon us an aggressive participation in the visual world. . . . On account of media a new construct [of the self] has arisen.[14]

All this has significant social consequences. A major study found that 15 percent of Poles are ashamed of their country and look down at

13. Han, *Disappearance of Rituals*, 17.

14. Sulima, *Powidoki codzienności*, 15–16.

patriotism in general; they rather feel European than Polish. Another 28 percent feel ambivalent.[15] However, in the survey that Furedi cites, 47 percent of Poles claim they would defend their country, which is rather high in Europe. Moreover, the latter statistic evidently crosses the major party lines—those ashamed of their country are mostly on the left, which in Polish party sympathy is rather small. In other words, all things considered a relatively strong sense of community was still to be found within the country. But the latter cited study was before the outbreak of the war with its genuine horrors, with the passage of time a later survey found a large group of approximately a third of Poles would wish to escape from their country, while a fairly small percentage would be willing to fight on account of relationship with its national community.[16]

Relationships with others are fostered in community. For Han rituals are symbolic acts that pass on, the values on which a community is based. Rituals are thus crucial for building community, while much in the neoliberal order, he claims, leads to the erosion of community. It is hard to say whether the neoliberal order is the only culprit, but certainly a number of the flaws Hans lists are present.

Polish society is quite interesting for consideration because it is at a crossroad. If we were to map it onto Han's schema, the seemingly most obvious course would be to present an until recently traditional society rich in community-building rituals that has been bludgeoned by the neoliberal order together with its accompanying economic processes which have largely transformed it. Among other things, Poland has moved significantly in the direction of a contemporary secular, atomized society—the statistic on those ashamed of being Poles is some indication of this. But it must nevertheless be stressed that Poland was only apparently a "traditional" society at the end of the Cold War. If the neoliberal order has indeed played a major role in the erosion of nourishing forces of community such as festivals—as opposed to "events" of a consumerist society—and rituals that allow it to flourish and develop an identity, then it can be said very similar and in some ways more powerful forces were confronted during its subjugation to the Communist system within a totalitarian state. During the Cold War, community was attacked by Communist collectivism, which also attacked religion, the major source of ritual. Why Poland exited that regime in a relatively healthy condition is a long story albeit some straightforward aspects

15. See Maciejewski, "Co zrobić z 'zawstydzonymi Polską?,'" 38–39.
16. Kozubal, "Sondaż."

are fairly well known, with religion playing a major role.[17] We will examine this aspect in depth later.

Through great effort the national community largely overcame the socially destructive forces of the Communist system aimed at atomizing Polish society, and thus significant traditional elements of the society were saved, especially if we compare it with neighboring post-Communist countries. And so these "traditional" elements had confronted and to a significant extent withstood a very modern and ruthless opponent. Now the situation is quite different, and community confronts a number of the seductive—rather than coercive, although there is a growing tendency in that direction—forces described by Han. And so community receives a certain stigma of "localism" in contrast to a globalist meritocracy, which has its political implications.[18] And community is a crucial force for working out the common good although it is not altogether successful in confronting those corrosive forces.

Another seminal element in Han's list of pathologies of the neoliberal society is the lack of closure, or at least a certain manner of closure. Culture is a positive form that aids in providing an identity for a community. Quite important in his reflections, culture is receptive to what is foreign. Despite its undoubted specificity, a national culture is not a closed vessel. And so Polish culture is obviously inclusive in Han's sense—basically drawing upon a broadly understood European cultural wealth, with some of its specificities more evident; historically, for instance, early on we see the Italian renaissance, evident in many buildings in older cities, while the more contemporary Italian neorealism influenced the Polish School of Film—most prominently in early films of Andrzej Wajda—just to give a couple of examples along the same cultural trajectory of creative incorporation. At a fundamental level we can speak of the Judeo-Christian tradition simultaneously drawing on the Greek and Roman traditions.

Globalization, on the other hand, creates a hyper-culture that perforates healthy boundaries and the natural attachment of people to sites. "A de-sited hyper-culture is additive" and thus hampers closure; what is more, it propagates "a cancerous proliferation of the same, even to the hell of the same," argues Han. This is one of the causes of the culture wars—although he does not use this term—since, as he puts it, "the strengthening of site

17. See, for instance, Weigel, *Final Revolution*.
18. See Kuź, "Globalism and Localism."

fundamentalism . . . is a reaction to hyper-cultural non-sitedness."[19] What he is referring to is the confrontation of radical nationalism with rootless cosmopolitanism. Needless to say the confrontation is hostile, and both sides are at fault to different degrees.

Certainly the Polish national community, at least at present, has a fairly strong sense of "sitedness." The forces of globalization have rather a transnational face largely in the form of the European Union. But Gerard Delanty has pointed out it is not so easy to define Europe as a political community since, despite efforts to the contrary, "it has become increasingly apparent Europe is not reducible to the EU any more than it can be explained as the sum of its national units. In short, Europe is a reality, but what kind of reality is it?"[20]

For a scholar, such a problem can be open-ended. For a Eurocrat, as we have seen, the solution is not always in line with the sovereign needs of national communities. And accession treaties are more and more frequently broken. Michal Gierycz, a Polish political scientist, set himself the task of coming up with a political anthropology of the national community in general in relation to the EU.[21] He hit upon using the key concepts from Thomas Sowell's book of 1987 *A Conflict of Visions*, in which the role of visions underpinning political ideologies is explored. Sowell argues social visions act as a kind of cognitive road map that guide everyone, since no mind can encompass social reality in its full dynamism and complexity. Crucially, when political leaders tap into broader social visions, they are able to create an agenda for both thought and action. Sowell focuses on two such broader contrasting visions that he persuasively argues have inspired politicians and influenced societies for the last centuries, the constrained vision and unconstrained vision of human nature. The constrained vision sees human nature as flawed and with a tragic bent, while the unconstrained vision is a moral vision that focuses on human intentions and ideals, and at times veers toward a dangerous utopian bent.

Upon presenting and critiquing Sowell's anthropological conceptions, Gierycz develops them further for his specific analysis plumbing the understanding of human nature in current European politics at the EU level. He argues European politics at the EU level fit into Sowell's unconstrained vision—one can say that this is additionally demonstrated through an

19. Han, *Disappearance of Rituals*, 34.
20. Delanty, *European Heritage*, 45.
21. Gierycz, *Europejski spór o człowieka*.

increasingly hyper-liberal agenda.[22] Conversely, he finds the constrained vision particularly useful for probing a national community. In his explication of a constrained anthropology on this basis he concentrates on what he takes as its underlying theological assumptions that interest him. Both in Sowell and in other contemporary political thinkers Gierycz detects an implicit assumption of the doctrine of the original sin through an awareness of the inherently flawed side of human nature. Yet although human nature has its limitations, he argues—following Sowell—taking this fact into account allows for organizing social matters in a more realistic and stable manner than would otherwise be possible. From a historical perspective Gierycz points out that even in Greek philosophy a constrained vision of the human being was present in the concept of natural law, which implied certain limits. The social nature of humans was also stressed, starting with the family and working upwards. From a similar time frame one could also go back to the famous debate between Saint Augustine and Pelegius as perhaps the earliest confrontation of the constrained and unconstrained view.[23] Later modernity largely went its own way with a greater stress on individualism but certain currents within it maintained a constrained anthropology to some degree; for instance, it can be detected among the contemporary communitarians. Some communitarians even praise such broad communal feelings as patriotism. Gierycz probes the theological underpinnings of Sowell's stress on the checks and balances necessary for the state, eloquently captured in James Madison's famous dictum: "If men were angels, no government would be necessary."[24]

The constrained anthropology that Gierycz proposes for the national communities clearly echoes Kaplan's tragic mind for a political community. Moreover, it is largely analogous to Han's positive closure that he locates in communities through culture and their siteness. The Polish national community also has a tradition that fosters an "including identity." In an interview John Paul II praised the Polish-Lithuanian Commonwealth in the late sixteenth century: a multinational and ethnic polity with a wealth of religious diversity, initiating a period of relatively harmonious coexistence uncommon in Europe at the time. As the Polish pontiff himself said of that golden era on another occasion, "For five centuries the Polish spirit

22. For a discussion of hyper-liberalism, see Gray, *New Leviathans*, chapter 3.

23. For a readable account of the dispute between Augustine and Pelagius, see Jacobs, *Original Sin*, 47–54.

24. Quoted in Madison, "Federalist 51."

of the Jagiellonian era prevailed. This made possible the emergence of a Republic embracing many nations, many cultures, and many religions." And he added optimistically, "All Poles bear within themselves a sense of this religious and national diversity."[25] Yet he was realistic enough to note that the tradition is not universally accepted within the current Polish national community. Nevertheless, this element of their identity has not completely disappeared. More importantly, this brings up the question of religion.

In *The Strange Death of Europe*, Douglas Murray astutely detects a palpable sense of ennui in the eponymous continent: the sense that "life in modern liberal democracies is to some extent thin or shallow and that life in modern Western Europe, in particular, has lost its sense of purpose."[26] Han's insightful essay suggests part of the roots of the continent's malaise, in no small measure related to the loss of religion, together with the rituals that hold a society together as a community. Murray felt the countries of Central Europe were something of an exception. To what degree was he right? As a vital country of the region undergoing a period of transition, Poland is worth looking at somewhat closer.

One might begin by noting that after the downfall of Communism in the seminal year of 1989, Polish society has quite rapidly elevated its standard of living, through its dynamic economy that fostered this change. Among of the secrets of the success of the transformation has the fact that Poland has remained largely oligarch free in contrast to a number of other former post-Communist countries as already mentioned. Moreover, local government reforms decentralized considerably more power to the local level, which "created a potential public counter-weight to any budding local oligarchs," as Krzysztof Mularczyk notes.[27]

However, another factor was a severe transformation that Han would describe in the broadest terms as incorporating a forceful version of neo-liberalism together with its system of production. A number of the pathologies he ascribes to this combination have gripped society, although they might not yet have taken quite the powerful hold he describes in his book; in the historically short period of time the socioeconomic system has been employed, the effects are nevertheless quite substantial. Will they continue to build up and—conversely—what forms of resistance to the erosion of

25. John Paul II, *Memory and Identity*, 87.

26. Murray, *Strange Death of Europe*, 258.

27. Mularczyk, "Poland Has Remained," para. 10.

community can be mustered are important to consider. Earlier we looked at some of the divisions in post-Communist countries.

To better understand the specific form of the challenge, in his perceptive study *Populism and the European Culture Wars*, Furedi points out that post-traditional and post-national sentiments, propagated by the likes of Jürgen Habermas, exercise substantial influence over the cultural elites and institutions of Western societies. This attitude tends toward specific aberrations; for instance, the author observes that the testimony to "the narrow technical vision of contemporary cosmopolitanism is that its worship of heterogeneity has contributed to the cultural valuation of parochial identity politics."[28] This might be understood as one of the political forms of the narcissistic cult of authenticity, and it has also substantially taken hold of political and cultural elites in post-Communist countries.

Among the last sources of ritual that remain in society is connected to one of the foundations of community: the family. Along with religion, the family was a target under Communism since it created more independent individuals better able to withstand regime propaganda. Many post-Communist societies are still affected by the decline of the family under Communism. Quite likely it is among the factors that make Russian society, with the family in terrible condition and divorce rates relatively high, not to mention the accompanying substance abuse, so susceptible and passive toward the authoritarian state propaganda of the Putin regime. One might add Russian society is hardly a model for Western conservatives that the dictator's propaganda claims it to be. The strength of the church in Poland—with the numerous accompanying rituals—was a crucial factor in maintaining the family. One significant critical study indirectly supports the notion that the strength of the family likewise helps in the EU.

It turns out that in Nordic countries, which are highly secular and gender equality is very high, much greater level of partner violence than in Poland was present. In the study *Violence Against Women: An EU-Wide Survey* published 2014, Scandinavian countries were at the top of the list for women reporting past abuse, ranging from 52 percent to 46 percent, while Poland was at the bottom with a couple of other countries at 13 percent.[29] It has been argued that the cause for this is likely connected with the high rate of cohabitation in Nordic countries: namely, relationships where partner turnover is comparatively rapid with all the heated

28. Furedi, *Populism*, 72–73.
29. Moynihan, "Nordic Paradox."

emotions involved. While religion is not mentioned as a reason for the low rate of abuse in Poland, it plays a role in the popularity of marriage, with all the incumbent benefits, to the couple and the community. How long this advantage will endure is another question.

As mentioned in the previous chapter, the largest community where trust is still largely possible according to Hosking is the national community. This is because despite the presence of a degree of anonymity, there are still institutions that are closer to the individual than in transnational societies, which are hardly communities. One could perhaps even go a step further, following Paddy Scannell, and see in trust a form of love—which he connects with communication and, we can add, is a key to community.[30] And so at this juncture we have a realistic channel to talk about love and the common good in relation to the national community.

The constrained view and presence of ritual in Poland come together at times to foster a tragic sense in its political community. In her book *Cross Purposes* Magdalena Waligórska points out there are two religious symbols that have bearing on the political imagination for Poles: the cross and the Virgin Mary. As she puts it:

> The uniqueness of the symbol of the cross in the political context . . . results from its simplicity, abstractness, and ease of reproduction and adaptation, as well as from its vertical expressivity and the variety of performative uses that it affords. . . . While the image of the Virgin Mary circulates in the Polish political context as a symbol much akin to, and, in some instances, functionally interchangeable with, that of the cross, it is the latter that offers a uniquely efficient tool for political mobilization, thanks to its visual minimalism, symbolic opacity, and wide range of affordances.[31]

This may be true at a certain level, but both symbols are community forming at a number of levels. Perhaps the most important ritual which powerfully unites the two symbols above are the stations of the cross, which traditionally take place each Friday during Lent. In the ritual, the "sorrowful mother," as the recited prayers put it, is at her son's side during the supreme tragedy. And this meaning of ritual is strengthened through Polish history, and adds to what might be termed the Polish tragic mind. At present we have the neo-imperialism of Russia and their invasion of Ukraine: that is, radical evil has returned to history just across the border from Poland. The

30. Scannell, *Love and Communication*, 14.
31. Waligórska, *Cross Purposes*, 22.

stations of the cross at this time unite many Poles in the sense of the tragic and in their prayers for Ukrainians: the political community in this way has been extended also on religious grounds.

A major support for political community is memory. A polity without memory is hardly a political community. If we look at the question of rituals and memory, then national holidays are a site where both meet in a national community. After 1989 Poles were able to celebrate their prewar holiday celebration of the recovery of the nation's independence after the end of the First World War, formally on November 11, 1918, which was not allowed under Communism. However, as of yet the authorities did not come up with compelling means of celebration, so after a time an NGO came up with a parade in Warsaw. Significantly, this highly overt patriotism was frowned upon in Europe. Bawer Aondo-Akaa, the son of a Polish Catholic mother and Nigerian father, attended an Independence Day parade in 2018 where there were a few extreme nationalist banners. When a Dutch politician making no distinctions called the entire parade fascist, this son of an African immigrant who declared himself a Polish patriot intended to sue the foreign politician for defamation. A pundit might retort, as Wróblewski did, defending the government for claiming the parade was patriotic, since it was, "after all, attended mainly by hard-working, middle-class people with families. They turned out, peacefully, in remembrance of getting our freedom after years of Russian and German occupation."[32]

Among the rituals of the Polish national community that supports memory in a more transcendent manner is the celebration of All Saints Day, a national holiday, when Poles visit cemeteries to honor their dead. In effect, albeit a holiday with religious roots, the ritual effectively unites believers and nonbelievers of the local—and national—community: quite often the graves of those who have served the local communities, and in major cemeteries, also the national community, are honored. Honoring the dead becomes a form of communion at a certain level, as does the history it evokes.

Considering a richer understanding of history as ritual and communion, we turn to Remi Braque's insight that the past is something with which "we can and should engage in conversation." The past has a responsibility toward us and vice versa. Conversely, "tradition is living transmission. . . . The past has made us. But, on the other hand, we to some extent make the past, we choose it as our own personal story, as leading us to where we

32. Wróblewski, "Poland: Patriotic, Not Authoritarian," para. 16.

are now."[33] Thus there is a dialogic sense of the past for us to attain, while dialogue is at the base of community. And historical memory is part of that dialogue, also at a moral level.

A necessary question to consider at this juncture is how far back can the memory of a national community go? Here we must also define what a national community is in terms of historical presence. One of the answers comes from the ethnosymbolists, of whom Anthony Smith is the most recognized scholar. That anthropological school seriously considers the existence of national communities as quite long standing. Moreover, among them are those who argue that in some cases they go back considerably further in time than the nation state, which is indeed a modern development, but is nevertheless developed on their base. Smith, for instance, argues that the origins and formation of nation can go quite far back in time, and so it is inappropriate "to tie their existence and formation to a particular period of history or the processes of modernization."[34] He even notes that some nations predate modernity. And in the case of Poland historical memory, a key component of national community, goes back over a millennium.

When Furedi proposes the recovery of historical memory for moral rearmament in the current critical period, he is implying the necessity of what has been called identity history without which community cannot flourish or cope with major challenges that have reemerged in out times. The division in Polish society discussed above also relates to the attitude toward memory. Ryszard Legutko notes how both the Communists and liberals denigrate the past ostensibly to augment progress. Thus for the apostles of modernity in his country "memory again became one of the main enemies."[35] Fortunately there are those who foster historical memory, at a number of levels, but we shall look more at a rather philosophical perspective—which includes religion—that unites memory with the present as it is potentially seen by Poles. This is among the keys for on the one hand maintaining, on the other preparing for the moral rearmament.

In their introductory comments to the double number of the yearbook *Political Theology* for the years 2021/22, entitled "From Salamis to Radzymin," the editors compared the two battles that represented major turning points: the Battle of Salamis, in which the Greeks defeated the Persian empire, and the Battle of Warsaw, in which the Poles defeated the aggressive,

33. Braque, *Curing Mad Truths*, 63.
34. Quoted in Giubernau and Hutchinson, "Introduction," 3.
35. Legutko, *Demon in Democracy*, 9.

newly formed army of the Soviet Union in 1920 that wished to make its first conquest beyond former Russian borders to the West. The battles were total in nature, that is turning points, Karłowicz and Cichocki argue, "simultaneously military, existential and civilizational conflicts." They add: "What comes to mind is that only states that respect human freedom can accomplish great things."[36] The issue was put together before the Russian invasion, but it was released when the war had already begun. In the promotion of the volume that took place live and online, the editors noted that Ukraine was now confronting a similar turning point in its existence.

In an issue of *Pressje*, a republican journal that was released when the war had begun, a similar comparison was made. Within the discussion about the vivacity of the nation state in an era of globalization, Nikodem Bończa-Tomaszewski noted that the Ukrainian war has elements of an inner conflict between two forms of Orthodox Christianity, which would essentially reduce it to a political conflict. Nevertheless, he insisted: "In my opinion the more accurate hypothesis is that . . . the year 2022 is the same for the Ukrainian nation as the year 1920 was for us [Poles]," and he further makes the point, "A consistent national ideology is coming into existence on account of the social sacrifice."[37] Thus, independently he came up with the same historical example, also demonstrating how historical memory brings Poles closer to the Ukrainian struggle.[38]

However, this similar philosophical reflection on historical analogies was derived from the surprising early successes of the Ukrainians against their powerful aggressive adversary. As the war continued and became even more devastating, the historical problem becomes more akin to the Second World War, which we shall come to shortly.

What is the importance of religion for national identity? Here historical events also play a role. Once again we turn to the editors of *Political Theology*. Cichocki is the author of a number of books richly treating political philosophy and theology. For instance, in his *North and South: Texts about Polish Culture and History* of 2018 he raises the question of the source of Polish and European culture.[39] Cichocki starts the introductory essay with the observation that so many Poles are placing their hopes in a unified Europe, which is not a problem in itself, but can nevertheless be an excuse for

36. Karłowicz and Cichocki, "Wolność," 9, 10.

37. Bończa-Tomaszewski, "Globalizacja się kończy," 165.

38. For a basic overview of the Polish-Soviet war, see Davies, *God's Playground*, 292–97.

39. Cichocki, *Północ i Południe*.

not examining themselves at a more profound level. Europe in its deepest sense has what he calls a north-south cultural vector, which was largely lost in the Enlightenment. He explains this symbolic orientation in that the origins of its civilization go back to the creative encounter of the barbarian peoples, that is the north, with Roman civilization, the south. This led to the conversion of the barbarian peoples which transformed their destructive force into a creative form. The key here is "conversion." Obviously there is the Christian dimension, but what was particularly meaningful was the impetus Augustine gave this conversion through overcoming the destructive force of Manichaeism. The influential Manichaeans believed in the reality of evil as a semi-divine force, while for Augustine evil is nothingness. Cichocki contends overcoming the nothingness of evil was a seminal factor in turning destructive forces toward the good. On account of their conversion and self-examination, each of the barbarian peoples including the Poles discovered their own version of the good, which resulted in the variety of the good in Europe.

Furthermore, the introduction to the ninth number of the *Political Theology* yearbook in 2016 celebrated the 1050th anniversary of Poland's first ruler accepting baptism, a foundational moment for the Polish national community. The founders of the think tank stated, "Catholicism is the source of the constant impulse for the universalization of Polishness, making it impossible for a descent into political and cultural particularism."[40] Significantly, the authors add, this leads to a sacramentally augmented feature of Polish politics: its inclusive nature. They claim the fact that since from the Catholic perspective faith stems from grace, freedom of religion is crucial to a sound political system. Cichocki and Karłowicz provocatively stress:

> If in today's [Polish] debates we return to the image of Jagiellonian diversity [i.e., more or less of the Polish Lithuanian Commonwealth] with its multi-ethnic, multi-religious and multicultural nature, then we must remember that Roman Catholicism facilitated rather than created barriers for it. From the Polish perspective a theocracy means an attempt at appropriating divine competence—it expresses the conviction that politics can impose faith. No state can be the ruler of the consciences of its citizens, otherwise it destroys the relationship of politics to the transcendent.[41]

---

40. Cichocki and Karłowicz, "Galeria Polaków," 8.
41. Cichocki and Karłowicz," "Galeria Polaków," 9.

As we have seen above, the Jagiellonian diversity was praised by John Paul II. Here a theological reason for its existence becomes discernible right from the foundation of the political community.

One of the questions the above raises is the problem of universalism. Yoram Hazony brings up this issue with his argument that "for more than a thousand years, the Roman Church . . . aligned itself, not with the ideal of setting the nations free as had been proposed by the Israelite prophets, but with . . . the aspiration of establishing a universal empire of peace and prosperity."[42] Pecknold likewise explores the complexity of this issue in his exploration of medieval political theology and its struggle with the problem of the relationship between the Pope and king.[43]

What led to such a positive solution to the issue in Poland? For one thing, the Polish monarch who accepted baptism aligned himself with the Pope rather that the nearby Holy Roman Empire. Moreover, since the papacy was quite distant, the Polish monarch and the developing church had a degree of independence. This remained the case when the eventual union with the Grand Duchy of Lithuania evolved into a republican commonwealth, with a strong Sarmation cultural base. In philosophical terms, as Ewa Thompson puts it,

> Sarmatism was a pre-modern Polish cultural episteme built on the belief that at the center of human endeavors reside metaphysical realities rather than the desire for power, and that all human concerns should play second fiddle to those realities. [Its] Christian articulation . . . provide the stimulus for Sarmation creativity. . . . Sarmatism is grounded in the idea of republicanism and is based on the virtue of the republic's citizens.[44]

The religious wars of the rest of Europe were essentially avoided. These may have had a great influence on the future evolution of the nation state,[45] but the situation was quite different in Poland, and remained so even when it lost its sovereignty in the eighteenth century. And that is why when Poland reemerged in a relatively multicultural state once again after the First World War and had to face the Soviet army in 1920; as Bończa-Tomaszewski puts it, "All the classes: the intelligentsia, peasants and workers, as well as Polish

---

42. Hazony, *Virtue of Nationalism*, 21.

43. Pecknold, *Christianity and Politics*, 51–68.

44. Thompson, "Sarmatism," 3.

45. See Pecknold, *Christianity and Politics*, 70.

Jews fought arm in arm against Russia."[46] As was the case at least in the September campaign when Poland was attacked by the Germans and Russians in 1939 at the onset of World War II.

After the war the minorities were essentially gone, through border changes, population transfers—including Poles from the former borderlands now transferred to the "allotted" new territories from Germany—and, of course, most tragically through the loss of the Jewish Poles at the hands of the Nazi German occupation. Roughly the same number of ethnic Poles and together with other minorities were killed during the—primarily German, but also Soviet—occupations, since, as Michael Steinlauf stresses, "nowhere else in Europe did the murder of Jews unfold amid such slaughter of the coterritorial people."[47] But the difference in the size of those populations meant the much greater tragedy of the Polish Jews, which has justly received much greater attention as well.

But at all points Poles fought, at home with a well-developed underground army and abroad; yet the considerable war effort against Hitler was not matched by any corresponding benefits relating to its future destiny. In his understanding of tragic realism Kaplan warns, "Fighting evil is a good, but it is also a good not to overextend your political and military capacities in the service of fighting it."[48] He gives the example of Franklin Roosevelt forming an alliance with the satanic Stalin in order to defeat the even greater evil of Hitler. But after this event, Polish "liberation" came at the hands of the Red Army and a new totalitarian state controlling the now largely ethnically homogenous Poland. Here we have the tragedy of the Central European "small nation" in Kundera's sense.

In her monumental *The Eagle Unbowed: Poland and the Poles in the Second World War*, Halik Kochanski recounts at some length the entire history of the Polish experience and effort during that seminal eponymous event. As a historian of Polish descent, one of the dramatic battles that she gives considerable attention is the Battle of Monte Casino in May 1944. This battle was a major turning point of the Allies Italian campaign toward the end of the war, where the German defenses that centered at the ancient Benedictine monastery were finally broken in a large part thanks to the effort of the Polish army, known as Ander's army after the general who commanded it. The army had been formed in the Soviet Union after the

46. Bończa-Tomaszewski, "Globalizacja się kończy," 165.
47. Steinlauf, *Bondage to the Dead*, 139.
48. Kaplan, *Tragic Mind*, 105.

Germans attacked their former ally and so the imprisoned Polish soldiers from that partition became "allies" but departed through Iran, after which they eventually joined the British forces in North Africa. Even the Germans paid tribute to their opponents. Here is a statement by one of their paratroopers stationed there: "They were brave soldiers. They were the bravest of all, in fact. . . . They looked at death but marched ahead nevertheless, which nobody else did. . . . This was a devastating thing—the order and sense of duty the Poles had. . . . We often couldn't believe it."[49]

In the cemetery at the site of the battle honoring the Poles who died doing their duty there are row upon row of crosses on a hillside. But among the crosses the occasional Star of David can be spotted, indicating the unity of the soldiers of different backgrounds—even among the "crosses" were likely a number of Protestant Poles. Among the Polish Jews who accompanied the army was Michał Waszyński, a popular and talented filmmaker during the interwar period, directing mainly Polish films, with the notable exception of The Dybbuk of 1937: a classic of Yiddish films.[50] He directed the film crew of Ander's army from the Soviet Union where it had been formed—among others creating a memorable documentary of the Battle of Monte Casino.

Poles present on various fronts fought for the freedom of the rest of Europe when the impossibility of their own homeland regaining its own freedom was virtually a foregone conclusion. "Your freedom and ours" was their motto: one that had served Poles for generations. But to make matters worse, no good deed goes unpunished: despite their efforts in serving the rest of Europe, their homeland would nevertheless lose its sovereignty for an additional half century, and many Poles would live in diaspora. Theirs was a tragic heroism. As for Waszyński, he became a successful Hollywood producer based in Italy, where he stayed, unlike many of his fellow veterans who mostly emigrated to the Anglosphere—many Poles likewise became successful after a fashion in their new homelands. But during the war the copies of The Dybbuk were destroyed by the Nazis or lost in Poland. Despite his efforts the director was never able to recover the film, and he did not survive to the time when the film finally saw the light of day and gained the

---

49. Kochanski, Eagle Unbowed, 475.

50. Paradoxically, Waszyński was fortunate to be in Lviv when the war broke out, where the Red Army invaded Poland and sent him to a Gulag, which quite possibly saved him from the Holocaust, since the Germans entered the city later.

recognition it deserved. Waszyński's misfortune is symbolic of the sense of loss many Poles experienced.

At this point the crucial question arises how many of the millions of Ukrainians who left their country will return to it once the war ends. Obviously, this partly depends on what will happen. But even with the best of possible outcomes in the war, a good number of them will remain abroad, not a few in Poland. To what extent will this diaspora create a resource for their compatriots at home? Polish historical experience in this matter suggests a considerable number of these Ukrainians will be a resource for those who have stayed in the devastated country. And, as mentioned above, some are already settling in Poland, thus close to their homeland. They have also formed a number of community—cultural and political—organizations. And among others there was a sizeable historical Ukrainian minority in the country that welcomed them as well.

But not all types of heroism were so tragic. As a young woman during the Second World War, Wanda Półtawska had been a Catholic resistance courier, which resulted in her being imprisoned at Ravensbrück concentration camp for passing messages to the Polish resistance against the Nazis. There, German doctors who wanted to see what would happen to bacteria under certain conditions injected diseased bacilli into her marrow, among other women. Since Poles were considered slaves by the aggressors they were ideal for such experiments. The needles the doctors used caused open wounds on their human victims and then they injected them with pus, causing the women agonies of fever and pain, often ending in a horrible death. Wanda had also "died" after four years at Ravensbrück. Or so the woman doctor thought when she looked at her motionless body. "Number 7709," she said. "Throw her on the pile." If a friend had not noticed her finger twitching on that pile that would have been the end of her.[51]

As has been pointed out, after what she lived through she knew the value of human life and dignity. But there is more to it than that. It has been indicated by thinkers such as Zygmunt Bauman that concentration camps were a product of modernity, thus they were hygienic and bureaucratic in their cruelty. Półtawska saw this and diagnosed it with accuracy in her memoirs. In an in memoriam piece by a columnist in a major Polish daily newspaper he pointed out that she was very straightforward with people. Despite the fact that Półtawska was religious, her soul mate was the late Oriana Fallaci, an atheist, but also pro-life. He quotes one of Italian

51. Esolen, "How the Church Has Changed."

journalist's essays: "The West is trundling through an intellectual and moral cancer. . . . The notion of changing or even distorting the roots of Life, dehumanizing it through the massacre of the weakest and even defenseless creatures. I mean: our unborn children, the future us."[52]

Półtawska faced this distorted modernity with her own dignity. While she was in the camp she vowed to God that if she survived, she would become a doctor: someone who healed people. Memories from the camp haunted her for years, but she earned her doctorate in psychiatry, and ministered especially to survivors of the camps, as well as to children who had been abused. In other words, she took her Hippocratic oath as a doctor very seriously, and unsurprisingly became strongly pro-life. Quite evidently, from early on after her recovery she practiced the moral principle that one must fight evil with good. Among her programs was helping doctors who were against having to conduct abortions group together in order to have their freedom of conscience in this matter honored, which even in a country with strong right to life protections was not always so simple—and even though it is among the human rights of the Lisbon Treaty of 2007 on the basis of which the European Union was reformed not so long after its formal creation in 1992.

Shortly after she started her medical studies in Kraków, Wanda and her husband became close friends with a young bishop in the city named Karol Wojtyła. No doubt radical feminists cringed at this, but John Paul II has been called a pro-woman pope by the prominent Christian feminist Elizabeth Fox-Genovese on account of his recognition of the special "genius" of women.[53] It is in no small measure thanks to his relations with women like Półtawska before he became pope that this intuition came about. But the point the columnist above was trying to make in comparing her to Fallaci was to intimate that the pro-life stance does not necessarily stem from a religious perspective, but from a truth about our humanity that religion seems more highly aware of. And that awareness also seems to be declining in Poland at present.

But the choices Wanda Półtawska made following her uncanny survival demonstrated the victory of the tragic mind over its challenges. Unfortunately, by the time she died—as a centenarian—not all Poles understood this.

52. Quoted in Maciejewski, "Synowie Medei, nasi bracia," 21.
53. Fox-Genovese, "A Pro-Woman Pope."

Kochanski notes that subsequent to joining the EU the attention of Poles is focused westward, rather optimistically concluding: "This return home has taken time, but now that Poland is once again free, the final chapter of the Second World War has at last been written."[54] As we have seen above, this is a somewhat simplistic conclusion.

But in both cases, the war and Communist totalitarianism, religion proved to be a key to surviving the new trials. At this point it is worth exploring what Poles learned during the period of Solidarity. The People's Republic of Poland was a Communist state which was supposed to represent the working class. The working class, however, had different ideas. Solidarity was the first successful workers strike in a Communist country, creating a union which was supposed to be redundant in a workers' paradise. But that was not the only irony of this revolution. Timothy Garton Ash summarized a key aspect: "It is hard to think of any previous revolution in which moral goals played such a large part; not only in the theory, but also in the practice of the revolutionaries; not only at the onset but throughout the revolution." But as the Communist state was also officially atheist, this bore fruit in an even greater irony, noted by the Polish philosopher Leszek Kołakowski: "It follows that the first workers' revolution in history was directed against a socialist state, and has proceeded under the sign of the Cross and the blessing of the Pope. So much for the irresistible laws of history discovered scientifically by Marxists."[55] Indeed, one of the first acts the striking shipyard workers in Gdansk in the summer of 1980 did was to fix a cross together with an image of Mary and Pope John Paul to the shipyard gates.

Although few could have predicted it, the 1980s were the last decade of Communist rule in Poland. The independent Solidarity movement played a prominent role in this, despite the regime's attempt to end its influence through a brutal martial law. The key here is "independent," since the totalitarian system fostered a monopoly on all forms of activity, especially from the working class which it claimed to represent in a special, materialistic manner.

The Catholic Church served the workers and society in this dark period. First and foremost through the inspiration of the Polish pope, but

54. Kochanski, *Eagle Unbowed*, 591.

55. The quote of Ash and Kołakowski are from Garbowski, *Religious Life in Poland*, 74, 73. For a basic history of the Solidarity movement and its results, see Davies, *God's Playground*, chapter 24.

he was served in the country by the clergy and laity. Few played a greater role in this sense than the chaplain of the Solidarity union at the Solidarity Congress in Gdańsk in September 1981, Reverend Józef Tischner, who delivered a number of sermons at key moments. These were gathered and expanded into the book *The Spirit of Solidarity*. Lech Wałęsa wrote an afterword to the English translation. He recalls discussing the lies of the regime and the propaganda it imposed on Poles for many years. About the book he writes, "The book recalls the meaning of words that in my country were deprived of their proper content by propaganda and given a totally different sense, an Orwellian one."[56]

And Tischner does indeed focus extensively on words in the slim, but fecund volume. He begins with a homily delivered at Wawel Cathedral on October 19, 1980, in which he points out: "History creates words in order that, in turn, they may create history."[57] In the sermon he concentrates on the word "solidarity," which indeed did make history. He starts with a straightforward question: "What does it mean to be in solidarity?" Drawing on the Epistle to the Galatians stress of reciprocally sharing burdens, Tischner explains: "It means to carry the burden of another person. No one is an island all alone. We are bound to each other even if we do not know it." Further along this line, he indicates the importance of conscience and creating bonds with the other: "Conscience is the foundation of solidarity, and the stimulus for its development is the cry for help from someone wounded by another human being. Solidarity establishes specific, personal bonds; one person joins with another to tend to the one who needs help."[58]

Solidarity is a moral ingredient of the good. Moreover, when politics is good, it also is suffused with the spirit of solidarity. Significantly, Tischner adds, "solidarity, the one that is born from the pages and the spirit of the gospel, does not need an enemy or an opponent to strengthen itself and to grow. It turns toward all and not against anyone."[59] In this manner he implies that solidarity—as important as it happens to be at this time of trial for Poles—is universal, and will be necessary even when the current travails have passed. Moreover, he indicates the universal does not eliminate the particular, whether that particular is personal or not. These particulars are in a sense illustrated by the additional words he explores in the book, such as

56. Tischner, *Spirit of Solidarity*, 105.
57. Tischner, *Spirit of Solidarity*, 1.
58. Tischner, *Spirit of Solidarity*, 9.
59. Tischner, *Spirit of Solidarity*, 3.

"art," "science," "exploitation," and "fatherland," to name a few, each receiving its own essay.

The liturgical sacrament of the word that inspires a number of the chapters ascends toward the ultimate sacrament, communion. Pecknold discusses how quite early Christianity revivified the Western political imagination through its understanding of the Eucharist as a powerful configuration of being itself and being in community.[60] Since the solidarity of the moment relates to a workers movement, Tischner explores the relationship of work to communion in the sermon he gave at the union's first congress, and which closes the book.

He starts the book with the importance of the history of words, he closes with the implications of the history of work. Where earlier people worked primarily with their family, "now the communion of working people has widened." This creates an enormous chain, bound by an ever broadening reciprocity. He makes use of geographical metaphors, the tributaries joining together in the main body of the river, but the river begins on high, specifically in the mountains. And it is the sacred liturgy of the Mass that encourages this. Tischner reminds those in attendance of the Mass as well as the readers of the book of the words that create the Eucharist, through the use of the "fruit of the earth and the work of human hands." Then comes the main point with which he concludes this part of the homily: "God does not come to us through the creation of nature alone, holy trees, water, or fire. God comes to us through the first creation of culture—bread and wine. Work that creates bread and wine paves the way toward God. But every work has a part in this work. Our work too. In this way our work, the work of each one of us, paves the way to God."[61]

The historical moment also has its meaning. Since so many hopes in Poland were pinned on the movement, together with understandable fears, the priest states, "The key question emerges, can we transform our Polish hopes into reality, especially the hope for wise and independent work?"[62] That was indeed a problem of the Communist system: that work was not independent. Tischner insisted work can only reach such a state when it is governed by the conscience of the worker and the bonds created with other workers. Under circumstances governing their lives this involved risk: "I believe that today we may lose everything, but if we succeed only

60. See Pecknold, *Christianity and Politics*, 16–29.
61. Tischner, *Spirit of Solidarity*, 97–98.
62. Tischner, *Spirit of Solidarity*, 100.

in planting the idea of independent Polish work in the human conscience we will have fulfilled our task."[63] Here he was aware of the risks that were involved in the movement, but insisted success could be measured by different means.

It can be seen solidarity in Tischner's teaching opened the way to what has been called a "politics of virtue."[64] John Milbank and Adrian Pabst try to develop the notion through challenging the liberalism of the West to be more humane, whereas Tischner is developing his version of the notion under the totalitarian constraints of Communism.

What specifically characterized Solidarity, according to Bronisław Wildstein, "was the sense of a communal interest, which resulted in the resignation from particular gains on behalf of the common good." He adds, "Solidarity was born the moment when the shipyard workers sacrificed what they were able to extort from the regime—and that was the latter fulfilling all their [negotiated during the strikes] postulates—in order to support all the others who joined their strike."[65] This choice had fecund results for the national community at the time.

Worth adding, Solidarity, especially from its having anchored itself in a deep axiological perspective, affects how more thoughtful Poles evaluate the current reality. Philosopher Dariusz Karłowicz, for instance, observes, "Reflecting upon the current state of Western culture demonstrates, that the divide between poverty and dignity has not been overcome. Europe dreams its consecutive dream of human self-sufficiency. There is no place for solidarity, because the solidarity of the gods of self-sufficiency is logically impossible."[66]

Zbigniew Stawrowski, a political philosopher who earned his PhD under the supervision of Reverend Tischner, gleaned the following political message from *The Spirit of Solidarity*. The structures of the good state should be open to all those who wish to help those who suffer: "In this manner politics and the state should be suffused and imbued with the spirit of solidarity."[67] In his writings he points out that the movement was inspired by John Paul II, especially through his first visit to Poland, which was attended by so many Poles that alongside his message they also saw

63. Tischner, *Spirit of Solidarity*, 103.

64. See Milbank and Pabst, *Politics of Virtue*.

65. Wildstein, *Bunt i afirmacja*, 530.

66. Karłowicz, "Miłosierdzie i solidarność," 20–21.

67. Stawrowski, *Solidarność znaczy więź*, 329.

themselves in a different—positive—context. The communal spirit that was suppressed under Communism.

But Solidarity also influenced the pope. Shortly before the union's congress in September 1981 he published his first social encyclical on the nature of work and the dignity of the worker, *Laborens Excercens*. George Weigel calls it "the most tightly focused social encyclical in the history of modern social doctrine."[68] Tischner quotes a poignant passage from the encyclical in his homily at the congress so soon after it was published: "Above all, work has the characteristic of binding people—this is the essence of its social power, the power of building a communion. Ultimately, those who work and those who govern the means of production or own them must somehow join with each other in this communion."[69] Weigel summarizes the combination of the pope's thinking and his experience of the trade union's flourishing: "During the 1980s, through their banned union and movement of national renewal, Polish dissidents had proclaimed that 'there is no freedom without Solidarity.' John Paul II extended that intuition by insisting that there can be no democracy without solidarity, the virtue."[70] Thus at that point the communion was with the workers and Polish society, upon which the Communist regime declared war through martial law. But the seed had been planted and ultimately it was the regime that was doomed.

The experience of Solidarity at its different levels is at a certain level what set Polish society apart from its counterparts in both the Soviet Bloc and Western Europe and generally the West. Serhy Yekelchyk sees knowledge of Solidarity and the generally rebellious Polish experience of Communism as having had a positive effect on Ukraine:

> Poland was so dangerous precisely because it was so close in terms of language and history. It has always been Ukraine's implicit alter ego, something we could have been, something we were not allowed to become. It was fitting that western Ukrainians, considered politically unreliable in Soviet times, had better access to Poland. Many travelled there, and many more could speak Polish fluently. But even in Russified Kyiv of the 1970s and early 1980s, Poland was often the topic of quiet conversations in kitchens. If Wałęsa could do it, maybe people's power was more than an empty slogan?[71]

68. Weigel, *Witness to Hope*, 420.

69. Quoted in Tischner, *Spirit of Solidarity*, 102.

70. Weigel, *Irony of Modern Catholic History*, 214.

71. Yekelchyk, "Homage to Poland," para. 3.

Ewa Thompson compares the experience of Solidarity with the events of May, 1968 in France. Coined a revolution—leading to the domination of an ethics of narcissistic authenticity with its devastating effect on community—it was led by Daniel Cohn-Bendit, significantly later a proponent of the federalist project of the EU. He received an honorary doctorate at an erstwhile Catholic university, despite his controversial earlier writings accepting pedophilia. Significantly, the May revolution was honored by the *New York Times* on its fiftieth anniversary in 2018, while Solidarity's fortieth anniversary a couple of years later was ignored by major media outlets outside of Poland.[72] Yet even in Poland younger generations have difficulty identifying with the movement and its values.

There's an oft quoted observation by Pope Paul VI: "Contemporary man listens more willingly to witnesses than to teachers, or if he listens to teachers, he does so because they are witnesses."[73] That is why witnesses of the movement such as Zbigniew Stawrowski—who was a young university student at the time—have an important task in keeping this memory alive. One of the critics of his work commented: "More than a philosopher or journalist he should be described as a 'witness.'"[74] He also calls the philosopher a thinker who continues the work of Tischner. This may be true at the philosophical level, but also institutionally: in 2003 Stawrowski was one of the founders of the Tischner Institute in Krakow.

The experience of Solidarity stayed with Stawrowski and imbued him with the mission to comprehend it to its depths and convey this to the generations that were not present. Among other things, he divides the experience of Solidarity into two main levels. The political level of the movement that confronted the "evil empire" of Communism, contributing to its downfall, another was the experience that transformed the participants. As one of those participants, he writes, "The experience was totally extraordinary. And so it is not surprising that scholars today who attempt to describe the period honestly, often enough resort to a category uncommon among them—to the category of the miraculous."[75]

However, it is important to understand some of the challenges Poles faced after 1989, from when they regained their sovereignty, to the early decades of the new century. Among other matters, Stawrowski's mission is

---

72. Thompson, "Solidarność 1980 w Polsce."

73. Quoted in Urbanczyk, "Teachers as Witnesses," para. 1.

74. Maciejewski, "Epifania czy nawrócenie wspólnoty?," para. 1.

75. Stawrowski, *Solidarność znaczy więź*, 293.

undergirded by such challenges. He himself points out some of the problems the Polish elite had at this turning point. For instance, the Communist past was not dealt with appropriately; this is one of the reasons, as we saw in the previous chapter, former Communists had such an easy time finding a place for themselves in the new reality. Stawrowski sees a certain betrayal of the ethics of solidarity in that instead of an attitude promoting service the elite turned to a form of paternalism or even disregard for the larger political community; moreover the nonviolent transition to sovereignty required coming to an understanding with the Communist regime, and consequently watered down the justice required to come to terms with their criminal past, and justice is one of the key elements of solidarity.

In 2020 Stawrowski published the second edition of his book *Solidarity Means Bonding, AD 2020*, in which a number of his philosophical studies and essays on the question of Solidarity and—most prominently—solidarity the virtue are explored. These essays were written over a number of years and cover his reflections on the writings of John Paul II on the topic, another section is on Reverend Tischner's thought on the subject, subsequently his own reflections on Solidarity primarily as a virtue are presented, and finally a section with essays on the problem of community in the face of its trials. The earliest piece is from 1994, the latest is from the same year as the book was published, which gives an indication how long the question has absorbed him. And since the various pieces include personal observations and reflections on current events—for instance, the dramatic plane crash in which President Lech Kaczyński died on route to honoring Katyń victims—the reviewer referred to above notes that, for this reason, "altogether his books can be arranged to provide consecutive parts of the autobiography and intellectual history of Poland in the last few decades."[76]

In the introduction to the first edition of the book, published a decade earlier and reprinted in the later one, Stawrowski related his experience with Tischner, whom he met briefly during the Solidarity period just before martial law, and with whom shortly afterwards he started his philosophical studies. For his mentor, the author reports, "Religion primarily means bonding."[77] And bonding is what Stawrowski stresses in the essay that was published in 2002 and which he used for the title of the book. In this he himself is a student of Tischner, as he explains that he was inspired

---

76. Maciejewski, "Epifania czy nawrócenie wspólnoty?," para. 1.

77. Stawrowski, *Solidarność znaczy więź*, 20.

by the homily that the latter gave during the Solidarity congress at Wawel Cathedral in October of 1980, and focuses on that virtue. Among the elements of solidarity he felt he had to come to terms with was that the first solidarity at the time the movement arose was an ethical community, while it later evolved into a community and became increasingly affected by politics in a negative sense.

In working through the meaning of solidarity and relying on his experience of the movement, he realized he had a moral imperative to present as faithful a description as possible from his position as a witness to one of the most important experiences of modern Polish history. And in order to do so he required the appropriate intellectual tools and points of reference. Crucial in this exploration was the dialogue with the thought of Tischner and John Paul II, without which it would not be possible to present those times from the most important perspective. The pope ignited the experience of dignity which spread like wildfire through Polish society, while the Solidarity chaplain provided the movement with a moral, intellectual framework. His means of doing so were reminiscent of a Socrates, who asked basic questions, like what is the essence of solidarity, the homeland, work, education, democracy? In creating the Solidarity movement there was a sense of a certain ethical sublimity, but thanks to Tischner's works, such feelings gained a measure of universality, both in a religious sense, as in a civilizing cultural measure. Participants knew then that the movement transcended who they were and as such had experienced an exceptional moment in the national history, and even of humanity.

In the introduction to the second edition Stawrowski noted how times had changed and Poles were now severely divided. He brought up Tischner's prophetic observation, that if the ethics of solidarity were ever given up it would be akin to the national community committing suicide. In these new dire times he asked the question, "Can the memory of the heritage of Solidarity still function as a foundation myth of our national community for young Poles, when one takes into account that the debate over what this heritage really means is now the source and simultaneously tool of divisions and conflicts?"[78] Significantly the part of the book with the essays that go beyond the impact of John Paul and Tischner on understanding solidarity was now called "Solidarity Is Still Before Us." It is in this part that the essay with the eponymous title "Solidarity Means Bonding" is now found.

78. Stawrowski, *Solidarność znaczy więź*, 10–11.

The essay was in the first edition of the book, since it is suffused with the long-standing attempt of Stawrowski to understand the virtue of solidarity that permeates the historical expression which he witnessed but that he felt also goes beyond this. This represents a necessary first step to taking Tischner's thought to a fuller level. One of the important things Tischner stressed is that solidarity does not require an enemy. Stawrowski does not abandon this notion, but transforms it to include a "negative" level as well as the obvious "positive" one. The negative level is the historical context of the time which the members of the community must rise above, to a greater or lesser extent. This negative community is the "political" community that initially confines the members. In the "first Solidarity," as it came to be known to Poles, this was the totalitarian state. And the author of necessity discusses the particular historical context of this specific political community. The true solidarity is the ethical community that is formed through virtue. This is not so different from what Tischner proposed, but the political context must be taken into account for a fuller understanding of the positive virtue. And in this context it is all the more remarkable that the ethical community came to the fore: "The special character of the solidarity community is primarily the fact that it was founded on the highest values, on absolute values."[79] Thus it was based on religious values, but these were ethical values, not confessional, so the community was inclusive, as is evidenced by its history.

One can detect a certain analogous relationship here in Stawrowski's understanding of the division of solidarity to Isaiah Berlin's distinction of positive and negative freedom. The political circumstances which hinder or help solidarity correlate to the question of negative freedom, while ethical solidarity is analogous to a positive freedom that includes responsibility: it is primarily this type of freedom that builds community, a community in which the members share each others' burdens. And Stawrowski does bring up the importance of freedom to build solidarity, which he defines as "a positive freedom, that fills the space of its actions, supports cooperation and builds community."[80]

Stawrowski feels the historical Solidarity movement accepted responsibility for Poland and held the conviction that the common good existed. This point was made in an interview published in the book, and his interlocutor consequently asks whether this respect for the common good

---

79. Stawrowski, *Solidarność znaczy więź*, 303,
80. Stawrowski, *Solidarność znaczy więź*, 342.

meant there was a republican perspective to the movement. He responds that a republican element can be discerned in Solidarity, but also considerably more: "The classical republican tradition is concerned with the public good, but primarily from the perspective of the political community."[81] Here he returns to the problem of the state and its role. The totalitarian state at the time of Solidarity and its aftermath until 1989 was anti-republican to an extreme, in sovereign Poland the state is not yet republican—if it ever will be, one can add.

Jan Maciejewski summarizes Stawrowski's thought on solidarity as a virtue as nearly prophetic and constituting a momentous task: the author encourages Poles "to understand what occurred more than forty years ago, not as a conversion, but an epiphany: a glimpse, a sign from another world, as a direction to follow. Not as a conversion in the strict sense understood in Western Christianity, but as a long, slow and arduous process."[82] Thus the moral rearmament of Poles has both its particular and universal dimension from this perspective.

However, epiphanies are not necessarily limited to the past. In an interview Stawrowski gave a couple of years after he published his thought provoking volume, similarly to Jan Rulewski he noted a spectacular rebirth of solidarity after the outbreak of the war in Ukraine. He claimed it was analogous to what happened when Solidarity was founded in 1980, and even called it "the second miracle of solidarity" with the difference that at that time solidarity spread in the Polish neighborhood, so to speak, while currently it was offered to the neighbors from the other side of the border.[83] Moreover, "Poles discovered solidarity among themselves, since the greater part of society had the same stance against the awesome injustice that Ukrainians experienced." He summarized this Polish experience: "Ukrainians escaping from the war entered our ethical world, bringing with them the image of demonic evil—metaphysical evil, that we thought our world had forgotten—and it simultaneously aroused within us deeply hidden levels of good. . . . The theological dimension of these events is extremely deep and I have the impression, that we are witnesses to the actions and struggles of tremendous spiritual powers present in our world."[84]

---

81. Stawrowski, *Solidarność znaczy więź*, 347.

82. Maciejewski, "Epifania czy nawrócenie wspólnoty?," para. 11.

83. Quoted in Grabias, "Wobec dwóch 'Solidarności,'" para. 10.

84. Grabias, "Wobec dwóch 'Solidarności,'" para. 26.

But Stawrowski also made certain to point out the profound level of solidarity that Ukrainians themselves are practicing at home: "It is the experience of solidarity of those, in which they risk their lives and die. The Ukrainians are already building their own, extremely powerful narrative of the experience of solidarity, which they experience among themselves in the face of the greatest imaginable injustice, in other words the criminal genocidal war."[85] And the Ukrainians are becoming aware of this. In an interview for a Polish religious weekly in June 2023 a month after the Kakhovka Dam was breached, causing extensive flooding and prompting mass evacuations, the bishop of Zaporizhzhia described the response in his diocese: "This war has instilled in us a great sense of solidarity. Everyone looks around to see what they can give to others, how they can help. Some bring necessary goods, others food, and other pass all these things further on. An entire network operates in order to bring the needy help as quickly as possible."[86]

Polish solidarity with Ukrainians also worked at different levels. There are accounts of various groups and individuals and their efforts. One dramatic account is quite illustrative of this effort: a young woman who did volunteer work with disabled Ukrainians in a city under attack, lost her leg when it was hit by shrapnel. She was taken back to Poland to receive an artificial leg, and soon returned to Ukraine to continue her work. She claimed that compared to what she witnessed in the war torn country, her experience was insignificant. In another instance, for a number of years a Polish foundation connected with Political Theology ran a day-care center in Mariupol. Tragically it was abandoned after the outbreak of the war and the siege of the city that took place right from the outbreak of hostilities: the defenders of the center actually lost their lives. On the think tank's website there is an account of all this that includes a statement by a ten-year-old child who was very fond of the center and had to escape from the city. She poignantly finishes her account, "More than anything else in the world I wish the war would end. I want to return to Mariupol, to see my grandma and hug her and my best friends. I'm certain in the day care center I will still paint the most beautiful picture of MY MARIUPOL."[87] The foundation managed to set a new center in a safer part of the country later that year.

85. Grabias, "Wobec dwóch 'Solidarności,'" para. 21.

86. Quoted in Zajączkowska, "Zanim woda odpłynie," 45.

87. Jednorożec, "Mój Mariupol," para. 7. The name is the child's pseudonym.

The statistics and the individual experiences of this solidarity with Ukrainians worked at numerous levels. Unsurpisingly, many refugees, especially children, needed help dealing with trauma and Polish NGOs have undertaken the task. At the broader statistical level, as Tomasz Wróblewski notes, "Nearly 6 million Ukrainians have passed through Poland, some two million have stayed for the long term." Despite this large number very few serious incidents have occurred between Poles and Ukrainians; what's more, "80 per cent of adult Ukrainians have taken full time jobs in Poland, pay taxes, rent or buy apartments, and statistically come into conflict with the law less often than Polish citizens. All this has been done without a single refugee camp, without separate zones for migrants, without nursing homes, or special schools for Ukrainian children."[88]

The above assessment is broadly correct, although problems do arise on occasion and it needs to be noted, after a year and a half of the war, according to a major opinion survey the percentage of Poles who accept the notion of Poland taking in more refugees had significantly dropped, but it was still approximately half the population. One can say epiphanies are extremely valuable, but they have their duration. Nevertheless they sometimes have lasting effects: the war and the Polish response to it also had a role in the strengthening the relationship between Poland and Ukraine at different levels, among them Serhy Yekelchyk poignantly claims, "Poland has always been Ukraine's advocate in Europe. Economic ties also developed, with large numbers of Ukrainians going to Poland as seasonal workers. Yet, this did not quite feel like joining Europe. But when millions of Poles accepted displaced Ukrainians into their homes, volunteered at train stations, and donated every spare zloty for Ukraine, this grand response truly made Ukrainians feel that they were back in the European family."[89] But what can be said about that European family?

When Poland entered the European Union, Poles were generally optimistic about the what awaited them. A Polish historian, and for a couple of decades the head of the Polish committee for UNESCO matters, put the issue in a historical perspective several years after the country was a member of the union. Regarding the problem of globalization that Europe faced after the first decade of this century, Jerzy Kłoczowski claimed, "It is obvious for all concerned that single European states are not capable of effectively dealing with the new challenges and strengthening the European

88. Wróblewski, "Poland Heads to the Polls," paras. 7–8.
89. Yekelchyk, "Homage to Poland," para. 6.

community constitutes the only solution. Wise compromises on the basis of the philosophy of subsidiarity, leaving a great range of national or regional autonomy are urgently needed."[90] This was a high end reflection of the general acceptance by Poles of their place in the European Union.

After the passage of time matters became more complex, and more conscious Poles began to think along different lines regarding their membership. Naturally there are differences of opinion, even from similar perspectives. I will keep to a broadly republican point of view, starting from a critical approach. For Stawrowski, soon enough it became obvious that solutions in the spirit described by Kłoczowski were generally not practiced in the EU, and the root of the problem was deeper than simply imperial politics with Poles at the periphery. One of the tendencies he criticizes in contemporary Western civilization is the tendency to approximate the Communist "permanent revolution." In the most general terms what this includes is a particular outlook on the world that is spreading, "with symptoms of a new 'Creeping' form of totalitarianism. A distinctive feature of this approach is the continuous reference to the basic values of the Western world, accompanied by a radical reinterpretation of them."[91] Others have noted something similar, at times associating it with ideas of the Altiero Spinelli, referred to as a founding father of the European Union, a Communist and federalist, who defined the earliest version of the superstate. For Stawrowski, human rights have become so numerous and cumbersome, on account of which the most important rights lose much of their weight. Reinterpretation is the case with the principle of religious freedom, where this crucial right becomes transformed into the freedom from religion.

In this instance Ryszard Legutko argues along similar lines concerning the infiltration of liberal democracy into religion. "Liberal democracy," he argues, "has an overwhelming tendency to politicize and ideologize social life in all its aspects, including those that were once considered private; hence, it is difficult for religion to find a place in a society where it would be free from pressure from liberal-democratic orthodoxy and where it would not risk a conflict with its commissars."[92] These two opinions could be taken as the belly aching of those who do not appreciate the new freedom their national community now had gained in the EU. However, it may be true as pointed out above that the opinions are a consequence

---

90. Jerzy Kłoczowski, *Nasza tysiącletnia Europa*, 213.

91. Stawrowski, *Clash of Civilizations*, 11.

92. Legutko, *Demon in Democracy*, 166.

of pondering the new political situation Poland now enjoys, but the complaints are akin to old ones pertaining to democracy such as the possible "dictatorship of the majority" or political theory as understood by Jacob Talmon, whom Stawrowski draws upon, who considered the possibility of the development of "totalitarian democracy." By the time the two Polish political philosophers wrote this, cancel culture, to give an example, had a strong presence in a good number of countries of the EU, and soon enough it crept into Polish liberal institutions. Along the lines of the constrained view of the political imagination we can go back to Lord Acton's observation that "power corrupts."[93] And when liberal democracy has power some form of corruption is inevitable. Even if some of the above criticisms are exaggerated, there is no system free from possible negative consequences. The Polish public intellectuals have noted particular ones.

At this point a particular problem that besets the Polish relationship with the European Union should be looked at more closely: the problem of the rule of law as a tool of normative imperialism. Stawrowski begins his analysis of the question from a philosophical perspective with a telling look at German Chancellor Olaf Scholz's address on August 28, 2022, at Charles University in Prague, where among others the politician praises the "fundamental values, enshrined by all of us in the EU Treaty, of human dignity, freedom, democracy, equality, the rule of law and defense of human rights."[94] He points out that in this platform text by the German chancellor, the noble ideas and values of the European Union are paradoxically brought together with undisguised threats of financial and political coercion towards noncompliant states, which are consequently accused of authoritarian inclinations. For Stawrowski, this is not surprising: "The selective application of the rule of law criterion within the EU has long been evident, with some states being harshly criticised for certain policies or institutional solutions, while others, typically the stronger states, are quietly left alone or regarded as irreproachable or even exemplary."[95] He goes on to demonstrate how this is hardly disguised. For instance, there is the case of the Venice Commission's opinion of January 16, 2020, on the condition of the rule of law in Poland. Among others in the opinion we learn that although in certain European countries judges are elected by the executive power, which in no way compromises their independence, the

---

93. Acton, "Lord Acton Quote Archive," para. 1.

94. Quoted in Stawrowski, "Rule of Law," para. 3.

95. Stawrowski, "Rule of Law," para. 4.

commission recommends that new democracies establish judicial councils because "such councils help in ensuring that the judicial community may make a meaningful input in decisions concerning judges." Stawrowski poignantly notes, "Leaving aside the ludicrous notion that new democracies should grant special political or power privileges to such a judicial community . . . it strikes one as a blatant disregard for the principle of equality among states." A fact of that inequality within the union is that most politicians accept it. This includes Polish politicians, the philosopher notes, "both those who find it unacceptable and protest loudly against it and those who have long since come to terms with it and are trying to find the best possible place for themselves in the current hierarchy in order to build their careers."[96] He quotes Jan Lewandowski, a member of the European Parliament from the liberal Civic Platform, who in an interview was asked about the problem and he simply responded, "Sometimes, the bigger one can do more."[97] One can add such double standards were also evident when a party with a liberal-left coalition replaced one with a conservative worldview in 2024 in Poland, Brussels turned a blind eye to the abuse of power in the post-election transition, demonstrating that favoritism trumps the rule of law.[98]

For all its brutality, Stawrowski finds a philosophical tradition behind this understanding of rule of law in the EU normative empire, going back to the tradition of Hobbes, and compares it to the understanding of the rule of law in Poland. He starts with the Polish tradition, which is more along the lines of the "state of law" as it was expressed in the nation's constitution of 1997: "The Republic of Poland shall be a democratic state ruled by law and implementing the principles of social justice."[99] The tradition that is drawn upon is the "state of law." This primarily pertains the noble tradition of natural law, in which legal acts gain their validity through their rational, just content. In such an approach, Stawrowski claims, "The rule of law means the rule of just laws. The rule of law emerges as identical to justice and is almost synonymous with it."[100] Such an understanding promotes a preferential option in favor of the poor, which among others it gained from Christian social teaching. What is common in Europe now and especially

96. Stawrowski, "Rule of Law," paras. 7–8.

97. Stawrowski, "Rule of Law," para. 6.

98. See Wróblewski, "What Is Happening in Poland," para. 5.

99. Stawrowski, "Rule of Law," para. 11.

100. Stawrowski, "Rule of Law," para. 13.

the EU, a different understanding of the rule of law is followed: "Instead of governance based on just principles and the absolute equality of all individuals before the law, with additional protection and care for the most vulnerable, there is a growing prevalence of a rule of law that favours the wealthiest and most powerful."[101]

Stawrowski explores how the rule of law in accordance with natural law evolved from Greek thought, which was developed by Augustine and especially Thomas Aquinas. As he puts it, "St. Thomas [follows] the lead of St. Augustine, for whom an 'unjust law is not law at all,' while states deprived of justice are no different from bands of robbers."[102] The rule of law in its more aggressive format stems from a tradition that goes back to Hobbes.

He summarizes the clashing views as with the point that current political disputes about the rule of law "whether in the context of the domestic order or interstate relations and their new forms that have emerged" within the European Union are merely the contemporary instantiations of the two visions of man described above: "One is represented by those who prioritize self-interest and perceive power as the ultimate determining factor, the other by those who know that a meaningful human life is permeated by a sense of community, solidarity and responsibility towards others."[103] It is obvious how in Stawrowski's philosophical interpretation of the rule of law he favors the tradition that works toward an ethics of solidarity and fosters the flourishing of community.

Among the broader political issues discussed at present in the country is the problem of an appropriate narrative to inspire Polish political and even economic policy or entrepreneurship. Among the more distinct proposals is one by Igor Janke, a member of a think tank that among other matters is engaged in training leaders. In his most recent book, *Polish Power* (2023), he insists Poland work on its potential to become a European power.[104] He introduces his book with an image of how depressing and hopeless Communist Poland seemed to him, and how dramatic the transformation has turned out on a number of fronts. He notes the country's current entrepreneurial dynamism which opens the opportunity for it to enter the major league in Europe: he includes an interview with Marcin Piątkowski, author of *Europe's Growth Champion: Insights from the Economic Rise of Poland*

---

101. Stawrowski, "Rule of Law," para. 14.

102. Stawrowski, "Rule of Law," para. 15.

103. Stawrowski, "Rule of Law," para 47.

104. Janke, *Silna Polski.*

(2018). Moreover, as an eastern flank NATO country during a time of war, successful in its role as a military logistics hub for the Ukrainians, its major per capita investments in defense will increase Poland's political clout and also result in economic growth through arms production that will follow. Tomasz Wróblewski, in turn, is the president of another prominent think tank, and personally has a relationship with the conservative American Heritage Foundation. In an interview concerning the expansionist and federalizing tendencies of the European Union and their meaning for Poland he brought up the question of the lack of a dynamic narrative that would allow the country to become a major player.[105] He insisted dynamic economic development would not continue without such a narrative. Among the potential avenues he felt was important was coming up with an inspiring narrative for the Three Seas Initiative: Poland played a major role in starting up this collaboration of East Central European countries, which—it is worth noting—is attractive enough that Greece requested to join in 2023. Being its initiator and largest member is not enough: Poland must come up with a narrative for the Three Seas Initiative to flourish, which in turn would aid in allowing the country to advance from its status as a medium player in the EU.

The narratives above are of a strategic nature, thus they are engaged in promoting a vision that might offer a political community a broader entrepreneurial or political—in some cases geopolitical—role that can be worked on. A key element of such narratives is that to the greatest extent possible they should neither be too farfetched or, conversely, too down to earth; that is, a balanced narrative is needed. Janke, for instance, points out that aside from Russia and Belarus, the neighboring countries are not the enemies of Poland; however, this is what must be kept in mind: "Everyone looks after their own interests, but we are all interconnected."[106] Thus a Polish strategy must be effective in such circumstance both from the perspective of its own interests and the interests of its potential partners. And depending on their nature on the outside they may have a soft power potential.

Since narratives are important for building community, Stawrowski also has his thoughts on the question, especially on the problem of the grand narrative. He takes on a number of academic views that are critical of such approaches from a philosophical perspective. He claims the postmodernist view that everything is relative is paradoxically itself a grand

---

105. Wróblewski, "Europa słabnie i zapada się."
106. Janke, *Silna Polski*, 33.

narrative, a view based on particular ideologies. Conversely, for Stawrowski national grand narratives are simultaneously universal and unique. They gain their universal nature through the civilization they represent. However, the problem is Western civilization is at war with itself and the powerful impose their own narrative on the weaker countries.

Stawrowski looks at some of the ironies of postmodernist liberalism, including how the idea of freedom on the one hand was taken to an individualistic extreme. Moreover, he is seriously concerned that "there are strong indications that the ideology that announces there is no single truth, likewise no objective criteria, that allows one to judge and condemn a criminal or totalitarian system, is itself preparing a consecutive, no doubt even more bitter form of totalitarian order then we have known until now."[107]

The above is why in response to this negative civilization, Stawrowski defines Poles by their religious heritage, since "the most important accomplishments of our thousand year history are consciously related to Christianity and confirm it as the most profound source of inspiration."[108] And so, despite the fact that not all Poles identify themselves with the religion, Poland is a Christian nation. Among the points Stawrowski stresses is that a grand narrative is not invented, it is defined by what a people stands for. He notes that in a sense Poles alongside their nation define the narrative. Memory defines a community, that is the role of history: it defines a national community's identity. Obviously not everything in that identity is unique; some nations have more similarities than other ones, some are quite far apart. What is exceptional about Polish identity in relation to other countries in Europe, Stawrowski maintains, "is that virtually right from the beginning of our history [it] has within it consciousness of what is best even in the political dimension, that is a classical vision of the republic as a model of a well organized community."[109]

Stawrowski is convinced that this Christian foundation of Poland is a key to its identity. If this is ever lost, it becomes a different country. Again, this is not a suggestion that everyone must be a Christian or even religious. It is fairly clear Stawrowski's grand narrative for Poland is intuitively based on a virtue ethics version of patriotism suggested by Alasdair MacIntyre, who argues that being born into a particular community is essential to our moral being. Virtues do not develop in a social vacuum:

107. Stawrowski, *Solidarność znaczy więź*, 418.
108. Stawrowski, *Solidarność znaczy więź*, 425.
109. Stawrowski, *Solidarność znaczy więź*, 425.

> *If* first of all it is the case that I can only apprehend the rules of morality in the version in which they are incarnated in some specific community; and *if* secondly it is the case that the justification of morality must be in terms of particular goods enjoyed within the life of particular communities; and *if* thirdly it is the case that I am characteristically brought into being and maintained as a moral agent through the particular kinds of moral sustenance afforded by my community, *then* it is clear that deprived of this community, I am unlikely to flourish as a moral agent.

This moral grounding involves a number of forms of civic virtues, among them those that are at the foundation of genuine relationships. MacIntyre stresses, "So patriotism and those loyalties cognate to it are not just virtues but central virtues."[110] Worth adding, few have demonstrated the patriotic virtues more heroically at present than Ukrainians confronting Europe's greatest trial in recent memory. Regardless of whether that heroic patriotic effort of the Ukrainians suffices to defend the country, their virtuous courage cannot be denied.

If we look beyond the Polish narrative at this point the question arises about the relationship between Polish memory, that is together with the Central European memory, and how it relates to the broader European memory. In the concluding chapter of the study *Europe Faces Europe: Narratives from its Eastern Half*, Swedish scholar Johan Fornäs raises an objection:

> When Estonia and other Baltic and East European countries achieved independence and opted for a "return to Europe," they did not erase the border between East and West. Instead, they moved it eastward by creating a new boundary between Europe and Russia as a new Eastern "Other." . . . If the Baltic States had just escaped Russian influence to reunite with the rest of Europe, the topic of freedom from oppression had the effect of raising a new curtain along Russia's western borders.[111]

This is the narrative of Central Europe as the European periphery that for the elite should be brought into order with the mainstream on their terms. When this example is looked at more closely, it is hardly believable that in a book published at the time of Russia's takeover of Crimea from Ukraine which one of its authors even refers to—not to mention the

110. MacIntyre, "Is Patriotism a Virtue?," 10–11.
111. Fornäs, "Euro-Visions," 193.

Chechen wars, and so on—such a claim would be found. The irony is that now Sweden itself has struggled hard to enter NATO.

A key to identity and community is naturally memory. This is articulated by John Paul II in the course of a book length interview: "Memory is the faculty which models the identity of human beings at both a personal and collective level. In fact, it is through memory that our sense of identity forms and defines itself in the human psyche."[112] At the collective level it is historical memory that bolsters identity, thus bolsters self-understanding. How does this memory work at present when so much has changed in Polish society? For instance, as Konstanty Pilawa notes, "A mere decade ago Poles used to migrate on masse to the West, currently it is to Poland that migrants come in great numbers from the East, also from the more distant East. They come here for the same reason we used to move to the British Isles or Germany: for prosperity and safety."[113] He adds Poland is now partly multicultural.

Some European societies have largely abandoned their past, leading to historical amnesia with all the connected problems Furedi describes. There is also a lack of patriotism which leads citizens away from the common good toward Han's narcissism of authenticity, often in a Hobbesian sense. This has been suggested as among the reasons why immigrant groups have trouble finding a place for themselves in these societies: societies are losing a sense of the self, so how can they share it with others? Rabbi Jonathan Sacks, for instance, in his book *The Home We Build Together* of 2007 criticized the dominant approach toward multiculturalism in his native Britain that essentially isolates immigrant groups depriving them of the notion of working toward a common good. And Britain was not alone in this failure: it has been suggested the radicalism of some immigrant groups in Europe possibly stems from this failure.

Poland's virtual mono ethnicity stems from the tragedy of the Second World War. Now that the situation is changing some have suggested studying the failure of countries such as France, Germany, and Sweden in this regard to learn from their errors. Wróblewski, for instance, has pertinently observed "multiculturalism as a state-building instrument, disconnected from shared values, is asking for disaster."[114] Pilawa further proposes that how the Poles see their national community needs rethinking. Similarly to

112. John Paul II, *Memory and Identity*, 144.
113. Pilawa, "Nieimperialne mocarstwo," 18.
114. Wróblewski, "Poland Heads to the Polls," para. 11.

Stawrowski, he believes that despite the strong secularization in the country, Poles should see their country in the tradition of Catholic social teaching as a natural community, which fosters the virtue of responsibility for the community, and simultaneously excludes an attitude of superiority over other ethnic groups. "For this reason," he insists, "Ukrainian and Belorussian minorities must be guaranteed full cultural autonomy. . . . A serious discussion on the status of the Ukrainian language in Poland together the public school education of the minorities closest to us awaits us."[115]

Pilawa is a member of a republican think tank, another member, Jan Filip Staniłko looks at the issue of an immigration policy and adds that Poland needs to make certain that immigrants are helped to feel at home in the country, in legal terms as well. He also agrees with Wróblewski that the Three Seas Initiative is one of the keys to the country's role in increasing strength in the EU, especially in matters of infrastructure and defense. He sees the controversial reforms within the European Union as necessary for it to maintain its competitiveness within the world, since it is sagging. He notes that "the EU is not actually sovereign and not many people think in that category." This, he insists, is a grave error. Staniłko favors a republican solution for the European Union from the perspective of an "institutionalized dispute about collective freedom."[116] There is no constitution in the EU, while the accession treaties are complex and obsolete in a geopolitical sense, and its enemies are interested in destabilizing it: "To endure, Europe must be sovereign, and to an increasing degree Polish sovereignty depends on European sovereignty."[117] European sovereignty must be part of the solution, but that likewise requires an understanding on the part of Brussels that the national communities are a treasure that enhances the EU and not polities to hold back. And after all, who would fight for Europe? Only the national communities stir up the patriotism for that sacrifice, and only a select group from among them at this point.

Ukrainians in their heroic struggle for saving their own sovereignty look to Europe and see their future within its bounds. As major archbishop of the Ukrainian Greek Catholic Church Sviatoslav Shevchuk puts it, Ukraine "wants to be a European country, because millions of Ukrainians saw a different world and came to the realization they no longer wish to

---

115. Pilawa, "Nieimperialnym mocarstwo," 21–22.

116. Staniłko, "Polska Piemontem Europy," 36.

117. Staniłko, "Polska Piemontem Europy," 36.

live the way they did."[118] Staniłko and Wróblewski argue that Polish sovereignty is related to its membership in the EU; however, Stawrowski also has a valid axiological point when he argues that there are two Europes, so the question is which Europe will Ukrainians chose once they are free to do so? No doubt the archbishop would align himself with the same one as the Polish philosopher: a Europe that is still based on religious values. In other words, a Europe that is still capable of creating a moral community, regardless of inherent differences. It would certainly be naive to say that membership in the European Union would be a solution to all problems; moreover, Ukrainians would have largely different problems, both internal and within the EU, than Poles had—and have: times have changed and will continue to do so.

It is nevertheless worth stressing in this respect how important religious tradition remains even at present if certain goals are to be achieved. Polish political philosopher W. Julian Korab-Karpowicz emphasizes the importance of religion in the public sphere, stating: "Although not everyone is religious, when considering a flourishing society the final end of humans should always be taken into consideration."[119] As Rabbi Sacks insists, "a life of immediate, unconstrained gratification" is in essence not worth living, to paraphrase Socrates. Sacks adds a significant cautionary point: "The only cultures that will survive into the future are those capable of making sacrifices for the future—for the future of their children and for generations to come." Thus, "One of the vital tasks performed by religion is to encode and preserve the wisdom of the past that would otherwise be forgotten, with disastrous results, in the present."[120] But what about the European civilization which is moving further and further away from this stance? Not to mention significant parts of Polish society are increasingly moving in a similar direction, especially among the young.[121] For one thing, it seems this leads to a view of the future that wishes to escape the past: here we unsurprisingly return to Furedi's culture of fear that is at the base of a society that is hardly prepared for dangerous times and lacking the moral foundations needed to face them adequately.

118. Quoted in Szewczuk, *Bóg nie opuścił Ukrainy*, 17–18. In the main text I use the English transcription of the author's name, which differs from the transcription in the cited Polish source texts; both are transcriptions from Cyrillic. The same is the case with a number of subsequent Ukrainian authors.

119. Quoted in Garbowski, "Principles of Social Harmony," 68.

120. Sacks, *Home We Build Together*, 214.

121. See Sikorski, "Nation (Still) Faithful."

We have seen above a significant part of the resources for the Polish struggle with moral rearmament. This has been viewed from a largely philosophical perspective—both political and, to some extent, theological—that takes into account historical memory and the European context in which the national community finds itself, with the war in Ukraine providing major additional stimulus for the enterprise and instilling it with a tragic sensibility that recognizes the agonizing decisions that at times must be taken. However, after a brief "epiphany" evoked by solidarity with suffering Ukrainians at the outbreak of the war, this rich resource continues to be ignored or rejected by more and more Poles.

A Conclusion for Dangerous Times

Deliver Us from Evil

FOR A SOVEREIGN STATE in dangerous times, rulers with a tragic sense are an asset for their political community, and one of the crucial sensibilities underpinning moral rearmament. Although he was writing a number of years before the war broke out in neighboring Ukraine, political philosopher Dariusz Karłowicz understands it in these terms: "A necessary condition of sovereignty is an awareness that the fate of political subjects is the conflict of rights and interests, and acting is inseparable from taking risks, which can be reduced, but cannot be eliminated."[1] Sovereignty is a freedom that carries with it enormous responsibility at all times, but especially in times marked with evil.

Regarding evil times, the tragic mind, according to Robert Kaplan, does not simply choose between good and evil, a relatively obvious matter, but must decide which is the lesser evil in order to reduce "the risk of catastrophes."[2] But the question is whether there is a lesser evil for the Ukrainians. For one thing it assumes the Russians wish to come to a compromise agreement, which is hardly certain. For another, some early agreement with the imperialist aggressors would require guaranties from Europeans in case of a renewal of aggression, which is more than likely, but the nations in the EU are quite far behind in rearmament, albeit slowly beginning to move somewhat in the right direction. Unfortunately, Kundera's tragedy of small nations cannot be excluded, which brings us back to the question of evil.

As Kaplan further puts it, "Guilt and conscience, which play a large part in the modern Christian West, are central to the realm of tragedy. And

1. Karłowicz, *Teby-Smoleńsk-Warszawa*, 33.
2. Kaplan, *Tragic Mind*, 102.

because there is such a thing as a guilty conscience, there is also evil, which requires one to overcome one's conscience."[3] Here Kaplan turns to Shakespeare's Iago, whom he regards as more diabolical than the biblical Satan. He adds in modern times an Iago-like character is Vladimir Putin.

Evil empires do not only affect invaded countries. A few years before the current war a Russian human rights activist complained that it was extremely frustrating for him to hear statements from abroad such as "Russians are not ready for democracy."[4] Yuri Dzhibladze pointed out that in the 1990s his people were quite pro-democracy. In other words, arguably the heaviest propaganda of the current regime has been aimed at Russians themselves: not to mention the dictator has purposefully turned so many of his young into cannon fodder. Putin with his entourage is effectively the Russians' greatest enemy: often enough his style of rule is compared to that of a mafia. It is hardly surprising a number of dissidents from the country who are abroad voice their support for Ukraine. Polish journalist Barbara Włodarczyk, who spent several decades in post-Soviet Russia, also remembers those times of promise and how they were swallowed up by Putin's renewed imperialism. There is no evidence they will return, but she keeps hoping for the conversion.

Among the Poles who have a good understanding of the theological aspect of the evil of the war, Filip Memches also stresses that the leading myth of the Russians to this day is the Great Patriotic War in which they defeated the Nazis.[5] In this sense the Russians identify themselves with the Soviets. As mentioned earlier, from the Polish perspective what is omitted in the myth is the fact that the Soviets were initially allied with the "evil" Nazis. From the Russian perspective, if the Nazis represented evil, identifying the Ukrainians with Nazis justified the war against them. This is to no small degree related to the political theology of the Russians, which has never been articulated, but Menches feels is implicit in their actions.

According to Memches Russian political theology is greatly distorted by Gnosticism, through the Manichaeism present in Russian Orthodoxy: "What I mean is the conviction that the world is really evil, and violence and war serve a manner of purification, a turning point. The ruler is permitted to use violence, because it serves the purpose of purifying the world,

---

3. Kaplan, *Tragic Mind*, 103–104.

4. Dzhibladze, "Let's Not Isolate Russia," 140.

5. Memches, "Polityczna teologia przemocy," 135.

which is at any rate evil. All that Patriarch Cyril does, fits in with this theology. Violence is sanctified."[6]

Memches notes this fits in with the long history of Caesaropapism that has afflicted the Orthodox church in Russia. Considering this servile stance the state expects from the church and its priests, the unexplained violent death of Alexander Men in 1990, an independent minded priest, is hardly surprising. The state is essentially above confessional religion, and fascism is evil. Memches sums up this line of interpretation: "Fascism is like an icon of evil, and it is Russia which fights with it, that is Russian political theology."[7] Some argue this fight with "fascism" is part of a Russian messianic sense, which the war with Ukraine bolsters. Memches sees Russia as a civilization that is cutting itself off from the West. In this he is not alone.

Ukrainians see Russian evil similarly to the Polish author. Major Archbishop Sviatoslav Shevchuk voices the broader consequences simply. He states, "Currently disinformation has become a weapon" and that "in the world of post-truth, truth is essential because lies kill." He perceptively intuits that "the reason for the war are internal diseases of post-Soviet Russia, which tries to solve these problems through external aggression."[8] And this aggression has no bounds. Civil society activist and Nobel laureate Oleksandra Matviichuk puts it quite pointedly: "Unpunished evil expands."[9] She lists the sites in which the Russian fight with "internal diseases" had militantly spread, from Chechnya, Georgia, Moldavia, and Syria, to name a few, before sinking so deeply and mercilessly into her Ukraine. Matviichuk pithily describes the struggle Ukrainians are involved in: "We are fighting for values which have no state borders. Such a value is freedom. Such a value is solidarity. We live in a complicated world and only by liberating it can we make it safer."[10]

In a particularly touching essay published in Poland, "Death and Eternal Life in Times of War," Mykhailo Dymyd, a scholar and priest of the Ukrainian Catholic Church, whose son was killed in the war, gives his stirring reflections on the invasion. He begins, "Physical death—on account of the aggressive war initiated by the Russian Federation and its president Vladimir Putin against Ukraine—is currently present in the Ukrainian and

6. Memches, "Polityczna teologia przemocy," 144.

7. Memches, "Polityczna teologia przemocy," 145.

8. Quoted in Szewczuk, *Bóg nie opuścił Ukrainy*, 9, 17.

9. Matwiczuk, "Musimy wygrać tę wojnę," 3.

10. Matwiczuk, "Musimy wygrać tę wojnę," 3.

Russian nations and can come in an extremely cruel fashion."[11] Among others he points out how important prayer is in the battle with evil. At the conclusion of his theological reflections on the current war, he addresses Christians everywhere, insisting they ask themselves, "What is my personal struggle? What is my personal victory over evil? . . . Whatever our current situation, each of us is called upon to 'proceed to our own front with Christian courage, to confront evil, and not simply wait somewhere behind the lines.'"[12] This raises the question, how do Poles confront evil?

For a number of ages now, drawing on its history Michał Łuczewski claims, "Central Europe is a bloodied altar."[13] Among others he draws on Carl Schmidts's notion of a global civil war, which appears to be surfacing, also within the Polish national community—despite the lessons the country's history offers on building an ethical community, one might add. Starting at a less apocalyptic level, a religious version of the tragic mind is the necessity of confronting the evil within, as Dymyd implies is our duty in whichever country we happen to be in. In Poland, this does not deny the genuine tragedy occurring in neighboring Ukraine, but likely if certain matters would be genuinely confronted within its own national community greater assistance could also be given to its neighbor, as is also evidenced by the conflicts between the two countries, despite their overall solidarity. This is a task for the political class but also includes the basic level of the national community and its desires. Marek Cichocki sites a report from a survey on the desires of ordinary Poles. These are fairly predictable, they desire a safe and peaceful country that is democratic and just: "That is only the beginning of the list, on which it is notable what ingredient is missing— strength."[14] The problem is in these dangerous times without strength there will be no lasting peace. Poles are equipping themselves for military defense, but inner conflicts remain. Then there is the problem of strength on the part of the broader European Union, since some members seem to have a limited understanding of this issue. And where it is growing it took some time to crystalize and even more to enact. But strength can be misdirected without the moral rearmament that Furedi intuits the West requires. In this

11. Dymyd, "Śmierć i życie wieczne," 59. The author was the first president of the Ukrainian Catholic University in Lviv.

12. Dymyd, " Śmierć i życie wieczne," 67.

13. Łuczewski, "Słowiańska teologia polityczna," 4–6.

14. Cichocki, "Spokój w niebezpiecznych czasach," A2.

context, Stawrowski's insistence of the necessity of a profound ethical community in Poland is more valid than ever, and valid for Europe as well.

In a manner that corresponds to this, Major Archbishop Shevchuk declares nothing could be worse than a false peace in the war. That would be counterproductive to a possible reconciliation between the Ukrainians and the Russians. What is necessary is a true conversion of the aggressor: "Without condemning the crime, without justice, reconciliation is not possible, because peace without truth and justice does not exist."[15] This desire for reconciliation after what Ukrainians have experienced is extremely noble and although it belongs to Christian morality that does not make it any easier. But quite likely it could only come about with the full defeat of the aggressor, not a very likely prospect. Here the West is partly to blame for now supporting the struggle enough. And of course Poles have good reason to side with the Ukrainians on this crucial point, even if part of the population is exhausted with the war and for the moment seems to have the luxury of such a stance. One of the Polish experts who has a comprehensive view of what such a victory over the evil empire signifies and how a false peace would affect East Central Europe and Western Europe concludes, "The effort goes beyond Ukraine itself and has a zero sum character: what the West loses, its enemies automatically gain. It's worth remembering this before we start repeating a capitulating narration."[16] To put it differently, moral strength and political determination is what Europe and more broadly the West also needs, as well rearmament. Because if Ukraine is not delivered from evil, where will it stop?

15. Quoted in Szewczuk, *Bóg nie opuścił Ukrainy*, 19.
16. Sokała, "Dajmy Ukrainie wygrać," M17.

Bibliography

Acton, Lord. "Lord Acton Quote Archive." Acton Institute, 2024. https://www.acton.org/research/lord-acton-quote-archive.

Anderson, Perry. *Ever Closer Union: Europe in the West*. London: Verso Books, 2021.

Applebaum, Anne, and Jeffrey Goldberg. "The Counteroffensive." *Atlantic*, Jun 2023.

Arestovych, Oleksii. "Zełenski uwierzył, że rządzi światem." Interview by Maciej Pieczyński. *Do Rzeczy*, Oct 23–29, 2023.

Ash, Timothy Garton. "Postimperial Empire: How the War in Ukraine Is Transforming Europe." *Foreign Affairs*, Apr 18, 2023. https://www.foreignaffairs.com/ukraine/europe-war-russia-postimperial-empire.

Auer, Stefan. *European Disunion: Democracy, Sovereignty and the Politics of Emergency*. London: Hurst & Company, 2022.

Auer, Stefan, and Nicole Scicluna. "Poland Has a Point about the EU's Legal Supremacy." *Politico*, Oct 19, 2021. https://www.politico.eu/article/poland-court-eu-legal-supremacy/.

Bailey, Riley, et al. *Russian Offensive Campaign Assessment*. Washington, DC: Institute for the Study of War and AEI's Critical Threats Project, 2023.

Baszczak, Łukasz, et al. *How Polish Society Has Been Helping Refugees from Ukraine*. Warsaw: Polish Economic Institute, 2022. https://pie.net.pl/wp-content/uploads/2022/07/Pomoc-pol-spol-UKR-ENG-22.07.2022-C.pdf.

Bielecki, Jędrzej. "O przyszłości Unii zdecyduje Ukraina." *Plus Minus Rzeczpospolita*, Jul 9–10, 2022.

Bielefeld, Ulrich, and Nikola Tietze. "In Search of Europe: An Interview with Jacques Delors." *Eurozine*, Jul 1, 2011. https://www.eurozine.com/in-search-of-europe/.

Bildt, Carl. "The Promise and Peril of EU Expansion." *Foreign Affairs*, Sep 28, 2023. https://www.foreignaffairs.com/europe/promise-and-peril-eu-expansion.

Bloxham, Donald. *Why History? A History*. Oxford: Oxford University Press, 2020.

Bończa-Tomaszewski, Nikodem. "Globalizacja się kończy, narody zostają." Interview by Kamil Wons. *Pressje* 61 (2022) 163-167.

Braque, Rémi. *Curing Mad Truths: Medieval Wisdom for the Modern Age*. Notre Dame, IN: University of Notre Dame Press, 2019.

Brzezinski, Mark. "Pomoc, którą wspólnie ofiarujemy nadaje znaczenia słowom *Sława Ukrajini*." *Wszystko Co Najważniejsze*, Jun 6, 2022.

Budzisz, Marek. "Pora na postawienie kwestii polsko ukraińskiego państwa federacyjnego: Potrzebne są odważne decyzje." wPolityce.pl, Jun 6, 2022. https://wpolityce.pl/swiat/601592-kwestia-polsko-ukrainskiego-panstwa-federacyjnego.

Burleigh, Michael. *The Best of Times, the Worst of Times: A History of Now.* London: Macmillan, 2017.

Caulcutt, Clea, et al. "When Will Europe Learn to Defend Itself?" *Politico*, Sep 27, 2022. https://www.politico.eu/article/emmanuel-macron-olaf-scholz-defense-europe-strategic-autonomy-ukraine-war/.

Cavanaugh, William T., and Peter Manley Scott. "Introduction to the Second Edition." In *The Wiley Blackwell Companion to Political Theology*, edited by William T. Cavanaugh and Peter Manley Scott, 1–11. Chichester, UK: Wiley Blackwell, 2019.

Cichocki, Marek. *Północ i Południe: Teksty o polskiej kulturze i historii.* Warsaw: Teologia Polityczna, 2018.

———. "Spokój w niebezpiecznych czasach." *Rzeczpospolita*, Oct 30, 2023.

———. *Walka o świat.* Warsaw: Państwowy Instytut Wydawniczy, 2022.

———. "Zaklęcia Brukseli już nie działają." *Wszystko Co Najważniejsze*, Oct 30, 2023.

Cichocki, Marek, and Dariusz Karłowicz. "Czym jest Teologia Polityczna." *Teologia Polityczna*, n.d. https://teologiapolityczna.pl/czym-jest-teologia-polityczna.

———. "Galeria Polaków." *Teologia Polityczna* 9 (2016) 7–9.

Coker, Christopher. *The Rise of the Civilizational State.* Cambridge: Polity, 2019.

Davies, Norman. *God's Playground: A History of Poland, Volume II; 1795 to the Present.* Rev. ed. Oxford: Oxford University Press, 2005.

Dębski, Sławomir. "Zachód bardziej boi się przegranej Rosji niż przegranej Ukrainy." *Wszystko Co Najważniejsze*, Jul 5, 2022. https://wszystkoconajwazniejsze.pl/slawomir-debski-zachod-bardziej-boi-sie-przegranej-rosjii-niz-przegranej-ukrainy/.

"A Declaration on the 'Russian World' Teaching." *Occasional Papers on Religion in Eastern Europe* 42.4 (2022) 121–27. https://digitalcommons.georgefox.edu/ree/vol42/iss4/11.

Delanty, Gerard. *The European Heritage: A Critical Re-Interpretation.* London: Routledge, 2018.

Delsol, Chantal. "Polska w obliczu szantażu." *Wszystko Co Najważniejsze*, Dec 14, 2021.

Dettmer, Jamie. "Key Weapons in Ukraine's Resilience: Ingenuity and Improvisation." *Politico*, Nov 20, 2022. https://www.politico.eu/article/vladimir-putin-volodymyr-zelenskyy-ukraine-russia-war-weapons-tactics/.

———. "The Toxic Legacy Putin Is Leaving Ukraine." *Politico*, Mar 24, 2023. https://www.politico.eu/article/toxic-legacy-vladimir-putin-war-ukraine/.

Dobrołowicz, Michał. "Nie zostawaj w domu, skróć dystans, pomóż." *Plus Minus Rzeczpospolita*, Mar 5–6, 2022.

Duda, Andrzej. "Przemówienie prezydenta Andrzeja Dudy w Radzie Najwyższej Ukrainy." *Salon24*, May 22, 2022. https://www.salon24.pl/newsroom/1228925,przemowienie-prezydenta-andrzeja-dudy-w-radzie-najwyzszej-ukrainy-caly-tekst.

Duranti, Marco. *The Conservative Human Rights Revolution: European Identity, Transnational Politics, and the Origins of the European Convention.* Oxford: Oxford University Press, 2017.

Dymyd, Michajło. "Śmierć i życie wieczne w czasach wojny." *Czterdzieści i Cztery. Magazyn Apokaliptyczny* 13 (2022) 58–68.

Dzhibladze, Yuri. "Let's Not Isolate Russia." Interview by Agnieszka Lichnerowicz. *New Eastern Europe* 2 (2016) 136–41.

Elefteriu, Gabriel. "Is the Ukraine War at a Turning Point? Zelensky and His Top General Paint a Grim Picture." *Brussels Signal*, Nov 17, 2023. https://brusselssignal. eu/2023/11/is-the-ukraine-war-at-a-turning-point-zelensky-and-his-top-general-paint-a-grim-picture/.

———. "Post-Ukraine, Everything Has Changed and There Is No Return to Normal: Reconfiguring the State to Deal with Recurring Crises Is Now a Matter of Survival." *Brussels Signal*, Jan 25, 2024. https://brusselssignal.eu/2024/01/post-ukraine-everything-has-changed-and-there-is-no-return-to-normal-reconfiguring-the-state-to-deal-with-recurring-crises-is-now-a-matter-of-survival/.

Esolen, Anthony. "How the Church Has Changed the World: Be Not Afraid." *Magnificat*, May 2020.

Fallon, Michael. "In Defeat, Vladimir Putin Is Becoming Desperate." *Telegraph*, Nov 17, 2022. https://www.telegraph.co.uk/news/2022/11/17/defeat-vladimir-putin-becoming-desperate/.

Fornäs, John, "Euro-Visions: East European Narratives in Televised Popular Music." In *Europe Faces Europe: Narratives from Its Eastern Half*, edited by John Fornäs, 181–235. Bristol: Intellect Books, 2017.

Fox-Genovese, Elizabeth. "A Pro-Woman Pope." *Christianity Today*, 1998. https://www.catholiceducation.org/en/controversy/feminism/a-pro-woman-pope.html.

Furedi, Frank. *How Fear Works: Culture of Fear in the 21st Century*. London: Bloomsbury, 2019.

———. *Populism and the European Culture Wars: The Conflict of Values between Hungary and the EU*. London: Routledge, 2017.

———. *The Road to Ukraine: How the West Lost its Way*. Berlin: De Gruyter, 2022.

Galeotti, Mark. *The Weaponisation of Everything: A Field Guide to the New Way of War*. New Haven: Yale University Press, 2023.

Gallon, Jeremie. "Europe's East Gets its Day." *Politico*, Jun 2, 2022. https://www.politico. eu/article/eastern-europe-economy-romania-lithuania-poland-geopolitics/.

Garbowski, Christopher. "The Polish Debate on the House of European History in Brussels." *The Polish Review* 64.4 (2020) 60–70.

———. "Principles of Social Harmony and the Wedding of Progress and Tradition." *The Polish Review* 64.1 (2019) 64–71.

———. *Religious Life in Poland: History, Diversity and Modern Issues*. Jefferson, NC: McFarland, 2014.

Ghodsee, Kristen, and Mitchell Orenstein. *Taking Stock of Shock: Social Consequences of the 1989 Revolutions*. Oxford: Oxford University Press, 2021.

Gierycz, Michał. *Europejski spór o człowieka: Studium z antropologii politycznej*. Warsaw: Wydawnictwo Naukowe Uniwersytetu Kardynała Stefana Wyszyńskiego, 2017.

Giles, Kier. "Russian Defeat Is More Dangerous than Russian Victory." In *How to End Russia's War on Ukraine: Safeguarding Europe's Future, and the Dangers of a False Peace*, 26–27. London: Chatham House, Russian Eurasia Progamme, 2023.

Giubernau, Montserrat, and John Hutchinson. "Introduction: History and National Destiny." In *History and National Destiny: Ethnosymbolism and Its Critics*, edited by Montserrat Giubernau and John Hutchinson, 1–22. Malden, MA: Wiley-Blackwell, 2004.

Głuchowski, Piotr. "Kto zdjął nogę z gazu. Czy po decyzji Gazpromu wrócimy do szczelinowania łupków?" *Wyborcza*, Apr 28, 2022. https://wyborcza.pl/duzyformat

/7,127290,28388928,kto-zdjal-noge-z-gazu-czy-po-decyzji-gazpromu-wrocimy-do-szczelinowania.html?disableRedirects=true.

Goodhart, David. *The Road to Somewhere: The Populist Revolt and the Future of Politics.* London: Hurst, 2017.

Grabias, Karol. "Wobec dwóch 'Solidarności': Rozmowa ze Zbigniewem Stawrowskim." *Teologia Polityczna*, Aug 30, 2023. http://teologiapolityczna.pl/zbigniew-stawrowski.

Gray, John. *The New Leviathans: Thoughts after Liberalism.* Dublin: Allen & Lane, 2023.

Gudziak, Borys. "Ukraiński opór rzuca wyzwanie narcyzmowi i relatywizmowi naszych czasów." *Wszystko co Najważniejsze*, Feb 11, 2023.

Gupta, Sarthak. "NATO Deems Russia as 'Terrorist State,' Calls for Support for Ukraine." *Jurist*, Nov 21, 2022. https://www.jurist.org/news/2022/11/nato-deems-russia-as-terrorist-state-calls-for-support-for-ukraine/.

Han, Byung-Chuk. *The Disappearance of Rituals: A Topology of the Present.* Translated by Daniel Steuer. Cambridge: Polity, 2020.

Hazony, Yoram. *The Virtue of Nationalism.* New York: Basic, 2018.

Hosking, Geoffrey. *Trust: A History.* Oxford: Oxford University Press, 2014.

Huston, John, dir. *The African Queen.* Written by John Huston et al. Horizon Pictures, 1951.

Ilves, Toomas Hendrik, and Radosław Dutczak. "Były prezydent Estonii: Rasizm wobec mieszkańców Europy Wschodniej jest politycznie poprawny." Klub Jagielloński, May 10, 2022. https://klubjagiellonski.pl/2022/05/10/byly-prezydent-estonii-rasizm-wobec-mieszkancow-europy-wschodniej-jest-politycznie-poprawny/.

Jacobs, Alan. *Original Sin: A Cultural History.* London: Society for Promoting Christian Knowledge, 2008.

Janke, Igor. *Siła Polski.* Warsaw: Czerwone i Czarne, 2023.

Janke, Igor, and Marek Budzisz, "Federacja, ścisła współpraca czy dystans? Bez Polski Ukraina przegrałaby wojnę." YouTube, Jul 7, 2022. https://www.youtube.com/watch?v=IoJCiabDOgw.

Janša, Janez. "The Political Processes in Europe Turned away from Democracy." Interview by Ferenz Almassy. *Visegrad Post*, Oct 6, 2022. https://visegradpost.com/en/2022/10/06/janez-jansa-the-political-processes-in-europe-turned-away-from-democracy/.

Jednorożec, "Mój Mariupol. Relacja dziesięcioletniej Żeni, która uciekła z oblężonego miasta." *Teologia Polityczna*, Feb 21, 2023. https://teologiapolityczna.pl/moj-mariupol-1.

John Paul II. *Memory and Identity: Conversations at the Dawn of a Millennium.* New York: Rizzoli, 2005.

Judt, Tony. *Past Imperfect: French Intellectuals, 1944–1956.* Berkeley: University of California Press, 1992.

Kamiński, Łukasz. "Not Only Putin Must Be Held Accountable, but Also Communism." *Wszystko Co Najważniejsze*, Mar 3, 2022. https://wszystkoconajwazniejsze.pl/lukasz-kaminski-not-only-putin-must-be-held-accountable-but-also-communism/.

Kamman, Samantha. "Hamas Positioned Rockets Next to Pool, Kids' Playground, Using People as 'Human Shields': IDF." *Christian Post*, Nov 7, 2023. https://www.christianpost.com/news/hamas-positioned-rockets-near-childrens-playground-idf.html.

Kaplan, Robert. "The Cost of Russia's Collapsing Empire." *Unherd Magazine*, Feb 7, 2024. https://unherd.com/2024/02/the-cost-of-russias-collapsing-empire/.

———. *The Tragic Mind: Fear, Fate, and the Burden of Power.* New Haven: Yale University Press, 2023.

Kari, Olha. "Siła dobroci i siostrzeństwa w mrokach wojny." *Wszystko Co Najważniejsze*, Nov 3, 2023. https://wszystkoconajwazniejsze.pl/olha-kari-sila-dobroci-i-sio strzenstwa-w-mrokach-wojny/.

Karłowicz, Dariusz. "Miłosierdzie i solidarność." *Teologia Polityczna* 10 (2017–2018) 15–21.

———. *Teby-Smoleńsk-Warszawa. O złudzeniu nietragiczności polityki.* Warsaw: Teologia Polityczna, 2020.

Karłowicz, Dariusz, and Marek Cichocki. "Wolność, porządek polityczny, religia." *Teologia Polityczna* 13 (2021–2022) 9–11.

Karnitschnig, Matthew. "Putin's Useful German Idiots." *Politico*, Mar 28, 2022. https://www.politico.eu/article/putin-merkel-germany-scholz-foreign-policy-ukraine-war-invasion-nord-stream-2/.

———. "The Truth about Germany's Defense Policy Shift." *Politico*, Feb 27, 2023. https://www.politico.eu/article/germany-zeitenwende-defense-spending-nato-gdp-target-scholz-ukraine-war-russia/.

Karnitschnig, Matthew, and Wojciech Kość. "Meet Europe's Coming Military Superpower: Poland." *Politico*, Nov 21, 2022. https://www.politico.eu/article/europe-military-superpower-poland-army/.

Kasianov, Georgiy. "The War over Ukrainian Identity: Nationalism, Russian Imperialism, and the Quest to Define Ukraine's History." *Foreign Affairs*, May 4, 2022. https://www.foreignaffairs.com/articles/ukraine/2022-05-04/war-over-ukrainian-identity.

Kirchick, James. *The End of Europe: Dictators, Demagogues, and the Coming Dark Age.* New Haven: Yale University Press, 2017.

Kłoczowski, Jerzy. *Nasza tysiącletnia Europa.* Warsaw: Świat Książki, 2010.

Kochanski, Halik. *The Eagle Unbowed: Poland and the Poles in the Second World War.* London: Allen Lane, 2012.

Kononczuk, Peter. "EU Has Given Poland €145m to Help with Ukraine Refugees." *Notes From Poland*, Oct 20, 2022. https://notesfrompoland.com/2022/10/20/eu-has-given-poland-e144m-to-help-with-ukraine-refugees/.

Krugman, Paul. "How Germany Became Putin's Enabler." *New York Times*, Apr 7, 2022. https://www.nytimes.com/2022/04/07/opinion/germany-russia-ukraine-energy.html.

Kundera, Milan. "The Tragedy of Central Europe." *New York Review of Books*, Apr 26, 1984.

Kuź, Michal. "Globalism and Localism in the Perspective of Polish Politics." Warsaw Institute, Jun 27, 2017. https://warsawinstitute.org/globalism-and-localism-in-the-perspective-of-polish-politics/.

Legutko, Ryszard. *The Demon in Democracy: Totalitarian Temptations in Free Societies.* New York: Encounter, 2016.

Libera, Antoni. "Widmo rozbioru trzeciej generacji." *Teologia Polityczna*, Mar 8, 2020. https://teologiapolityczna.pl/antoni-libera-widmo-rozbioru-trzeciej-generacji.

Lough, John. *Germany's Russia Problem: The Struggle for Balance in Europe.* Manchester: Manchester University Press, 2021.

Lovett, Ian. "For Years, Poland Warned of the Russian Threat. Now, the West Is Listening." *Wall Street Journal*, Mar 24, 2022. https://www.wsj.com/articles/for-years-poland-warned-of-the-russian-threat-now-the-west-is-listening-11648140891.

Łuczewski, Michał. "Słowiańska teologia polityczna." *Czterdzieści i Cztery. Magazyn Apokaliptyczny* 13 (2022) 4–34.

Maciejewski, Jakub. "Co zrobić z 'zawstydzonymi Polską?'" *Sieci*, Nov 13–19, 2023.

Maciejewski, Jan. "Epifania czy nawrócenie wspólnoty? Wokół książki Zbigniewa Stawrowskiego *Solidarność znaczy więź AD 2020*." *Nowy Napis Co Tydzień*, Jun 24, 2021. https://nowynapis.eu/tygodnik/nr-106/artykul/epifania-czy-nawrocenie-wspolnoty-wokol-ksiazki-zbigniewa-stawrowskiego.

———."Synowie Medei, nasi bracia." *Plus Minus Rzeczpospolita*, Oct 28–29, 2023.

MacIntyre, Alasdair. "Is Patriotism a Virtue?" Lecture presented for the Lindley Lecture, Lawrence, KS, 1984. https://kuscholarworks.ku.edu/handle/1808/12398.

Madison, James. "Federalist 51." Bill of Rights Institute, n.d. https://billofrightsinstitute.org/primary-sources/federalist-no-51.

"Madrid Summit Declaration." North Atlantic Treaty Organization, Jun 29, 2022. https://www.nato.int/cps/en/natohq/official_texts_196951.htm?selectedLocale=en.

Manent, Pierre. *Democracy without Nations: The Fate of Self-Government in Europe*. Translated by Paul Seaton. Wilmington: ISI, 2013.

Marek Kozubal, "Sondaż: Co zrobiliby Polacy, gdyby Rosja zaatakowała?" *Rzeczpospolita*, Dec 20, 23. https://www.rp.pl/wojsko/art39596581-sondaz-co-zrobiliby-polacy-gdyby-rosja-zaatakowala.

Matwiczuk, Ołeksandra. "Musimy wygrać tę wojnę na poziomie wartości." Interview by Michał Kłosowski. *Wszystko Co Najważniejsze*, Jul 18, 2023.

Melkozerova, Veronika "How I Decolonized My Russian Mind and Retook Kyiv." *Politico*, Oct 5, 2023. https://www.politico.eu/article/how-i-decolonized-my-russian-mind-russia-ukraine-history-education/.

Memches, Filip. "Polityczna teologia przemocy: O Rosji, wojnie i chrześcijaństwie." Interview by Michał Łuczewski. *Czterdzieści i Cztery. Magazyn Apokaliptyczny* 13 (2022) 135–49.

Michta, Andrew. "Russia's Invasion of Ukraine Is Transforming Europe." *19FortyFive*, May 8, 2022. https://www.19fortyfive.com/2022/05/russias-invasion-of-ukraine-is-transforming-europe/.

———. "What Happens after Vilnius Will Matter More Than the Summit Itself." *Wszystko Co Najważniejsze*, Jul 18, 2023. https://wszystkoconajwazniejsze.pl/andrew-a-michta-what-happens-after-vilnius-will-matter-more-than-the-summit-itself/.

Milbank, John, and Adrian Pabst. *The Politics of Virtue: Post-Liberalism and the Human Future*. New York: Roman & Littlefield, 2016.

Minder, Raphael, and Laura Pitel. "Poland and Germany: The Feud at the Heart of Europe." *Financial Times*, May 2, 2023. http://www.ft.com/content/81825290-29a2-48b2-8e69-73e897dafe9d.

Moynihan, Carolyn. "A Nordic Paradox: Higher Gender Equality, More Partner Violence." *Mercator*, May 28, 2019. https://www.mercatornet.com/a-nordic-paradox-higher-gender-equality-more-partner-violence.

Mularczyk, Krzysztof. "Poland Has Remained Largely Oligarch Free. This Is the Secret of Its Success." *Brussels Signal*, Dec 4, 2023. https://brusselssignal.eu/2023/12/the-secret-of-polands-success-is-the-avoidance-of-oligarchy/.

Murray, Douglas. *The Strange Death of Europe: Immigration, Identity, Islam*. London: Bloomsbury, 2017.

Myers, Fraser. "Donald Tusk Is No Friend of Democracy." *Spiked*, Oct 16, 2023. https://www.spiked-online.com/2023/10/16/donald-tusk-is-no-friend-of-democracy/.

Nowak, Andrzej. "Granice Europy." *Do Rzeczy*, Jul 11–17, 2022.

———. *History and Geopolitics: A Contest for Eastern Europe*. Warsaw: Polish Institute of International Affairs, 2008.

———. *Powrót Imperium Zła. Ideologie współczesnej Rosji, ich twórcy i krytycy (1913–2023)*. Krakow: Wydawnictwo Literackie, 2023.

———. "The West Is the Key to Ensuring that the Russian Imperial Reconquista Is No Longer Effective." *Wszystko Co Najważniejsze*, Jun 6, 2022. https://wszystkoconajwazniejsze. pl/prof-andrzej-nowak-the-west-is-the-key-to-ensuring-that-the-russian-imperial-reconquista-is-no-longer-effective/.

Panke, Julian. "The Fallout of the EU's Normative Imperialism in the Eastern Neighborhood." *Problems of Post-Communism* 62 (2015) 350–63.

Pecknold, C. C. *Christianity and Politics: A Brief Guide to the History*. Eugene, Oregon: Cascade, 2010.

Piatkowski, Marcin. *Europe's Growth Champion: Insights from the Economic Rise of Poland*. Oxford: Oxford University Press, 2018.

Pietrasik, Kamil. *Uchodźcy czeczeńscy w Polsce w latach 1994–2000*. Warsaw: Difin, 2022.

Pilawa, Konstanty. "Nieimperialne mocarstwo." *Pressje* 62 (2023) 16–23. https:// klubjagiellonski.pl/wp-content/uploads/2023/12/pressje-62-pdf.pdf.

"Poland Welcomes 4.62 Million Refugees from Ukraine." PolskieRadio, Jul 8, 2022. https://www.polskieradio.pl/395/7784/Artykul/2996236,Poland-welcomes-462-million-refugees-from-Ukraine-officials.

Pourchot, Georgeta. "EU's Eastern 'Empire.'" In *Revisiting the European Union as Empire*, edited by B. Behr and Y. A. Stivachtis, 17–31. London: Routledge, 2016.

Przeciszewski, Marcin. *Kościół w Polsce 2023. Teologia Polityczna*, Sep 26, 2023. https:// teologiapolityczna.pl/marcin-przeciszewski-kosciol-w-polsce-2023.

Rohac, Dalibor. "It's Time to Bring Back the Polish-Lithuanian Union." *Foreign Policy*, Mar 26, 2023. https://foreignpolicy.com/2023/03/26/its-time-to-bring-back-the-polish-lithuanian-union/.

———. *Towards an Imperfect Union: A Conservative Case for the EU*. Lanham, MD: Roman & Littlefield, 2016.

Roszkowski, Wojciech. "What Happened to European Values?" *Wszystko Co Najważniejsze*, Apr 12, 2022. https://wszystkoconajwazniejsze.pl/prof-wojciech-roszkowski-what-happened-to-european-values/.

Rulewski, Jan. "Warto mieć takiego sąsiada." Interview by Eliza Olczyk. *Plus Minus Rzeczpospolita*, Mar 26–27, 2022.

Sacks, Jonathan. *The Home We Build Together: Recreating Society*. London: Continuum, 2007.

Sandel, Michael J. *The Tyranny of Merit: What's Become of the Common Good?* London: Allen Lane, 2020.

Scannell, Paddy. *Love and Communication*. Cambridge: Polity, 2021.

Shablinsky, Ilya. "It's the Same Old Story from Putin." *Rights in Russia* (blog), Oct 12, 2023. https://www.rightsinrussia.org/shablinsky-32/.

Shortt, Rupert. *Does Religion Do More Harm Than Good?* London: SPCK, 2019.

Shriver, Lionel. "How the West Plays Up to Putin's Caricature." *Spectator*, Aug 2023. https://www.spectator.co.uk/article/how-the-west-plays-up-to-putins-caricature/.

Sikorski, John. "A Nation (Still) Faithful to Its Roots? What St. John Paul the Great Might Say to Poland Today." *Public Discourse*, Feb 5, 2024. https://www.thepublicdiscourse. com/2024/02/92572/.

Słojewska, Anna. "Co najbardziej grozi Europie." *Rzeczpospolita*, Sep 6, 2017.

Słojewska, Anna, and Jaume Duch Guillot. "Jak mamy myśleć o dziejach Europy." *Plus Minus Rzeczpospolita*, Oct 7–8, 2017.

Snyder, Timothy. *The Reconstruction of Nations: Poland, Ukraine, Lithuania, Belarus, 1569–1999*. New Haven: Yale University Press, 2003.

———. "The War in Ukraine Is a Colonial War." *New Yorker*, Apr 28, 2022. https://www.newyorker.com/news/essay/the-war-in-ukraine-is-a-colonial-war.

Sokała, Witold. "Dajmy Ukrainie wygrać." *Gazeta Dziennik Prawny*, Nov 10–12, 2023.

Sonnenfeld, Jeffrey. "Poland Was Right: Today You Are a Model for Others." *Wszystko Co Najważniejsze*, Sep 24, 2023. https://wszystkoconajwazniejsze.pl/jeffrey-sonnenfeld-polands-pivot-away-from-russian-gas-a-model-for-central-europe/.

Staniłko, Jan Filip. "Polska Piemontem Europy." Interview by Konstanty Pilawa. *Pressje* 62 (2023) 32–40. https://klubjagiellonski.pl/wp-content/uploads/2023/12/pressje-62-pdf.pdf.

Staniszewski, Mariusz. *Polska wojna kulturowa*. Warsaw: Warsaw Enterprise Institute, 2021.

Stawrowski, Zbigniew. *The Clash of Civilizations or Civil War*. Krakow: Tischner Institute, 2013.

———. "The Rule of Law as a European Value. The Philosophical Context of the Prevailing Political Dispute." *Wszystko Co Najważniejsze*, Oct 19, 2023. https://wszystkoconajwazniejsze.pl/zbigniew-stawrowski-the-rule-of-law-as-a-european-value-the-philosophical-context-of-the-prevailing-political-dispute/.

———. *Solidarność znaczy więź, AD 2020*. Krakow: Państwowy Instytut Wydawniczy, 2020.

Steć, Michał. "Rzeczpospolita Narodów Polski i Ukrainy?" Klub Jagielloński, Jul 2, 2002. https://klubjagiellonski.pl/2022/07/02/rzeczpospolita-narodow-polski-i-ukrainy-raczej-partnerstwo-oparte-na-interesach/.

Steinlauf, Michael. *Bondage to the Dead: Poland and the Memory of the Holocaust*. Syracuse, NY: Syracuse University Press, 1997.

Sulima, Roch. *Powidoki codzienności: Obyczajowość Polaków na progu XXI wieku*. Warsaw: Wydawnictwo Iskry, 2022.

Szabo, Christopher. "Why Have the Russians Been so Brutal in Ukraine?" Mercatornet, Apr 27, 2022. https://www.mercatornet.com/why-have-the-russians-been-so-brutal-in-ukraine.

Szewczuk, Światosław. *Bóg nie opuścił Ukrainy. Abp Światosław Szewczuk w rozmowie z Krzysztofem Tomasikiem*. Kraków: Wydawnictwo WAM, 2023.

Thompson, Ewa. "Sarmatism, or the Secrets of Polish Essentialism." In *Being Poland: A New History of Polish Literature and Culture since 1918*, edited by Tamara Trojanowska et al., 3–29. Toronto: Toronto University Press, 2019.

———. "Solidarność 1980 w Polsce vs. maj 1968 we Francji." *Teologia Polityczna*, Jan 18, 2021. https://teologiapolityczna.pl/ewa-thompson-solidarnosc-1980-w-polsce-vs-maj-1968-we-francji-felieton-1.

Tischner, Józef. *The Spirit of Solidarity*. Translated by Marek Zaleski and Benjamin Fiore. San Francisco: Harper & Row, 1984.

Tishkov, Valery. *The Russian World—Changing Meanings and Strategies*. Washington, DC: Carnegie Endowment for International Peace, 2008. https://carnegieendowment.org/files/the_russian_world.pdf.

Tismaneanu, Vladimir. *The Devil in History: Communism, Fascism, and Some Lessons of the Twentieth Century*. Berkeley: University of California Press, 2011.

Tokarski, Jan. "Bitwa o Europę." *Rzeczpospolita Plus Minus*, May 13–14, 2023.

Trofimov, Yaroslav. *Our Enemies Will Vanish: The Russian Invasion and Ukraine's War of Independence*. London: Penguin, 2024.

Turk, Žiga. "'Ever Closer' Union or 'Ever Stronger' Union?" Euractiv, Apr 14, 2022. https://www.euractiv.com/section/future-eu/opinion/ever-closer-union-or-ever-stronger-union/.

Umland, Andreas. "Russia Must Be Held to Full Account for Its Aggression." *Politico*, Nov 29, 2023. https://www.politico.eu/article/russia-held-full-account-aggression-invasion-war-crimes-ukraine-vladimir-putin-sanctions/.

Urbanczyk, Aaron. "Teachers as Witnesses." *The Catholic Thing*, Dec 3, 2009. https://www.thecatholicthing.org/2009/12/03/teachers-as-witnesses/.

Waligórska, Magdalena. *Cross Purposes: Catholicism and the Political Imagination in Poland*. Cambridge: Cambridge University Press, 2022.

Weigel, George. *The Final Revolution: The Resistance Church and the Collapse of Communism*. Oxford: Oxford University Press, 1992.

———. *The Irony of Modern Catholic History: How the Church Rediscovered Itself and Challenged the Modern World to Reform*. New York: Basic, 2019.

———. "What Ukraine Means." *First Things*, May 2023.

———. *Witness to Hope: The Biography of John Paul II*. New York: HarperCollins, 2001.

Weiler, Joseph. "Przedmurze chrześcijaństwa." Interview by Andrzej Godlewski. *Gość Niedzielny*, Jun 5, 2011.

Wildstein, Bronisław. *Bunt i afirmacja. Esej o naszych czasach*. Krakow: Państwowy Instytut Wydawniczy, 2020.

Wisse, Ruth. "Zelensky the Jewish Hero." *Commentary*, May 1, 2022.

Woziński, Jakub. "Wojenny rachunek dla Polski." *Do Rzeczy*, May 9–15, 2022.

Woś, Rafał. "Poland, Germany and the Fight for the Soul of the EU." *Spiked*, Aug 5, 2023. https://www.spiked-online.com/2023/08/05/poland-germany-and-the-fight-for-the-soul-of-the-eu/.

Wróblewski, Tomasz. "As Poland Heads to the Polls, the Parties Are Deeply Divided—but Not on How to Deal with Migration. The Polish Way Has Lessons for all of Europe." *Brussels Signal*, Oct 13, 2023. https://brusselssignal.eu/2023/10/as-poland-goes-to-the-polls-the-parties-are-deeply-divided-but-not-on-how-to-deal-with-migration-the-polish-way-has-lessons-for-all-of-europe/.

———."Europa słabnie i zapada się: Musi się poszerzyć, żeby liczyć się na świecie." Interview by Patrycjusz Wyżga. YouTube, Oct 29, 2023. https://www.youtube.com/watch?v=NozSxhCScZ8.

———. "Poland: Patriotic, Not Authoritarian." *Politico*, Mar 12, 2017. https://www.politico.eu/article/poland-patriotic-nationalist-not-fascist-pis-government/.

———. "What Is Happening in Poland Is Setting a Dangerous Precedent for the Whole of Europe: Autocracy in the Name of Liberalism Is Coming to a Parliament Near You Soon." *Brussels Signal*, Jan 11, 2024. https://brusselssignal.eu/2024/01/what-is-happening-in-poland-is-setting-a-dangerous-precedent-for-the-whole-of-europe-autocracy-in-the-name-of-liberalism-is-coming-to-a-parliament-near-you-soon/.

Yekelchyk, Serhy. *Conflict in Ukraine: What Everyone Needs to Know*. Oxford: Oxford University Press, 2015.

———. "Homage to Poland." *Wszystko Co Najważniejsze*, Feb 25, 2023. https://wszystkoconajwazniejsze.pl/prof-serhy-yekelczyk-homage-to-poland/.

Zajączkowska, Beata. "Zanim woda odpłynie." *Gość Niedzielny*, Jun 25, 2023.

Zarycki, Tomasz. *Ideologies of Eastness in Central and Eastern Europe*. London: Routledge, 2010.

Zielonka, Jan. *Counter-Revolution: Liberal Europe in Retreat*. Oxford: Oxford University Press, 2018.